EVENTS
THAT CHANGED THE
WORLD

EVENTS THAT CHANGED THE WORLD

igloo

igloo

Published in 2011
by Igloo Books Ltd
Cottage Farm
Sywell
NN6 0BJ

www.igloo-books.com

ISBN 978-0-85780-018-3

2 4 6 8 10 9 7 5 3 1
B044 0711

Author: Michael Heatley

Printed and manufactured in China

CONTENTS

INTRODUCTION

"Everything flows and nothing stays," said the Greek Heraclitus in around 500 BCE. For him, change was the fundamental truth underlying everything that is caught up in the flow of time.

History is a testament to that philosopher's insight. Every day societies and individual lives across the globe are shaped and reshaped in small and large ways. Fashions come and go, famine gives way to plenty, monarchs and governments are swept away, science provides us with technologies that our ancestors would have seen as magic, discoveries are made, wars are won and lost. As Tennyson later put it, 'The old order changeth, yielding place to the new.'

The world is in a constant state of flux – but every so often events occur that have a vastly more profound effect than the everyday shifting tides of politics and progress. Since we invented the wheel there have been certain moments on which history itself has turned. Some of them – like the moon landing of 1969 – were immediately recognised as great stepping stones in the history of humankind, witnessed by millions of people. At other times – for example the day that a bunch of geeks launched a new computer program – it is only when we look back that we can see the moment as pivotal. However, whether it was Christopher Columbus sighting the New World, setting in motion events that would lead to the rise of a great superpower, or a young man called Elvis Presley making a disc that would redefine popular culture forever, such moments have reverberated down the centuries. In a great domino chain of cause and effect, they have changed the world in ways that the people involved could never have imagined.

In these pages are descriptions of 100 events that have shaped the world we live in. Some have flowed from the act of putting pen to paper with an idea, such as Charles Darwin's Origin of Species. Other moments have taken place behind the closed doors of little-known laboratories. Still more have taken place before humanity's fascinated gaze on television, or, like the World War II D-Day landings, have involved the lives and deaths of thousands. Not all represent change for the better: the Wall Street Crash caused untold misery in the United States and around the globe, and the terrible events of September 11, 2001, have cost countless more lives than those of the people trapped in the World Trade Center that day. And the sinking of the Titanic and the explosion of the Challenger space shuttle are tragic reminders of human fallibility.

But the events in these pages also show our ability to achieve great feats, such as conquering the world's highest peak and reaching out into space, and our ingenuity in making leaps of scientific progress. Moments such as Live Aid in the summer of 1985 demonstrate the depth of human generosity and our willingness to be moved to great acts of compassion. And the election of the United States' first black president only 53 years after Rosa Parks was arrested for refusing to vacate her seat on a bus for a white man, serves to remind us how rapidly progress can happen: how quickly events can change the world.

Left: Nearly 3000 people died in the fateful attacks carried out in the USA on September 11, 2001.

Above: The famous New York skyline before the attacks occurred. At the time of their completion, the twin towers were the tallest buildings in the world.

Right: The World Trade Center south tower burst into flames after being struck by hijacked United Airlines Flight 175 as the north tower burned following the earlier attack.

9/11 TERRORIST ATTACKS

NEW YORK, USA
SEPTEMBER 11, 2001

By the time the ceremonial ribbon was cut in 1973, the World Trade Center had become one of the most recognizable sites in the world. Located in lower Manhattan, the World Trade Center could be seen for miles, its two towers gleaming more than 1,300 feet over New York City. That all changed on September 11, 2001. During the morning of that sunny late-summer's day, terrorists hijacked two airplanes and flew them into the towers, shocking a city, a nation and the world.

September 11, 2001 started like any other day as thousands gathered in lower Manhattan to begin their day. The sky was a crisp blue and the temperature was a very pleasant 70 degrees.

At around 8 a.m., two airliners took off within minutes of each other from Boston's Logan Airport on a cross-country journey to Los Angeles. A third flight left Newark, N.J., at around the same time on its way to San Francisco. A fourth passenger jet from Washington's Dulles International Airport left at around 8:10 a.m., for Los Angeles. All of the flights were loaded with jet fuel.

As Manhattan settled into its daily routine, American Airlines Flight 11 from Boston to Los Angeles unexpectedly changed its flight path over upstate New York and headed south towards New York City. Onboard were 81 passengers and 11 crew members. No one on the ground had any reason to suspect terrorists had taken control of the plane.

Flight 11 flew toward New York City - its new hijacker-pilot using the Hudson River as a road map. As the aircraft got closer, it began losing altitude. Two onboard flight attendants called the American Airlines reservation desk to let them know what was happening. Another attendant called the flight services manager at Logan Airport. She gave airport officials the seat numbers of the hijackers.

At 8:46 a.m., one of the hijackers, Mohammed Atta, flew Flight 11 into the north tower of the World Trade Center. The Boeing 767 sparked a huge explosion on impact, killing everyone on board and sending New York into chaos. It was the beginning of the worst attack on the United States since Pearl Harbor, six decades earlier, and the bloodiest day in American history since the Civil War battle of Antietam in 1862.

At 9:02 a.m., United Airlines 175 out of Boston smashed into the second tower, its image captured by news cameras and photographers. The plane carried 56 passengers and nine crew members. As the plane slammed into the building, a fireball erupted as glass and metal rained from the sky. The crash sucked desks, chairs, computers, and other debris out of the tower. Anyone who thought the first crash was an accident didn't think that any longer. America was under attack.

AT A GLANCE

The two airliners flown into the twin towers of New York's World Trade Center on September 11, 2001, struck at the very heart of the USA, destroying an iconic landmark and killing almost 3000 people.

21

Left: Rescue workers removed Father Mychal Judge NYC Fire Department Chaplain, from one of the World Trade Center towers.

Below: The Pentagon, following the attack. Everyone on board the airline and 125 people on the ground were killed.

At the time the second plane hit the tower, President George W. Bush was being introduced to a class of second-grade students at Emma E. Booker Elementary School in Sarasota, Florida. Just as he was getting ready to pose for pictures with the children, Bush's chief of staff Andrew Card informed the president about the attacks.

The terror was not over. The first wave of the attack, which hit the heart of America's financial system had happened. The second wave, which took aim at America's military and political center, was underway.

At 8:56 a.m., American Airlines flight 77 from Dulles disappeared from the radar screen. Air traffic controllers frantically tried to radio the pilot, but had no luck. Officials believed the plane had crashed. They soon realized the plane had been hijacked. As Flight 77 neared Washington, D.C., it increased its air speed just across the Potomac River in Virginia to 530 miles per hour, and ploughed into the Pentagon.

The plane carved a V-shaped wedge into one side of the building. Panicked office workers rushed outside. Smoke billowed from the wreckage. In addition to the 56 passengers and six crew members on board, 125 people on the ground were killed. Within minutes, rescue workers arrived to treat the wounded and search for bodies in the rubble.

Meanwhile, as United Flight 93 out of Newark passed south of Cleveland, Ohio, it took a sudden and violent left turn, and began flying southeast toward Washington. The hijackers forced the 38 passengers and seven crew members to the back of the plane.

As the plane continued on, the passengers and crew members used the plane's air phones to report the hijacking. They were shocked to learn about the other plane crashes. People on board realized that Flight 93 was part of the terrorist attack and believed, rightly so, that Washington was the next target. They decided to fight back.

Flight 93 soared over woodlands and cattle pasture. The passengers huddled with one another trying to figure out what to do. They voted to retake control of the plane. They stormed the cockpit and wrestled with the hijackers. The plane rolled upside down before crashing in a field in western Pennsylvania. Everyone on board died. Had the flight stayed aloft a few seconds longer, it would have plowed into a nearby school, housing 501 students.

In New York City, the devastation continued. The massive fires that raced through the twin towers weakened the heavy steel beams that held up the structures. The buildings collapsed in a storm of fire, dust and debris. A 10-story pile of twisted metal and ash scattered across 15 blocks in lower Manhattan. Passersby tore off their shirts to make bandages for the wounded.

Meanwhile, President Bush was aboard Air Force One and fighter planes were in the air ready to shoot down any more hijacked airliners. The plane's TV monitors were tuned into the local news stations that carried the devastation live. President Bush watched as the second tower collapsed. For security

reasons, the president did not return to Washington until later that night.

On the ground, New York City Mayor, Rudolph Giuliani took charge. He arrived on the scene moments after the second tower was hit. He watched in horror as people jumped from open office windows. The city was unable to use its emergency command center, which was inside the World Trade Center. Instead, the mayor and his aides set up a command post at a nearby firehouse.

Ordinary Americans, who had seen the tragedy unfold on television, were sickened. Yet, a gritty resolve emerged from the ashes, as Americans from all across the political spectrum and lifestyles came together in a show of hardened patriotism.

AT A GLANCE

As the smoke billowed in New York, Pennsylvania and outside Washington, a dark cloud covered the nation. The attacks sparked outrage across the globe.

Above: Workers removed tons of twisted wreckage from the site.

Right: Rescue teams came from every state to help recover the bodies.

People began flying American flags from their front porches. Major League Baseball players stitched American flags to their uniforms and thousands donated to relief funds to help the victims of the attacks.

To help recover the bodies, an army of construction workers, rescue teams, and ordinary citizens streamed into New York. They came from every state. Some stayed for just a few days, others much longer.

The workers removed tons of twisted wreckage. The job was so dangerous that people wrote their names and phone numbers on their arms to make identification of their bodies easier if the debris tumbled on top of them.

Workers removed portions of the building one hand bucket at a time as they looked for survivors. By the end, workers removed more than 108,000 truckloads of debris. The clean up went on 24 hours a day, seven days a week. Officials said cleaning up the site would take a year. It took eight months. However, five years later, workers were still finding human bones on the site.

People demanded an independent review on the genesis of the 9/11 attacks. At first, the Bush administration opposed any independent examination. Administration officials feared such an inquiry would be a distraction from defending the nation against future threats. Eventually, President Bush acquiesced and appointed an independent board to investigate.

The National Commission on Terrorist Attacks upon the United States, also known as the 9-11 commission, was established on Nov. 27, 2002. Its final report was issued on July 22, 2004. Commission members and staff interviewed more than 1,200 people in 10 countries. They looked at video footage of the hijackers passing through airport security and listened to cockpit voice recordings.

Chaired by Thomas H. Kean and Lee Hamilton, the commission concluded that while the 9/11 attacks were a shock, "they should not have come as a surprise." Commission members said that Islamist extremists had given plenty of warning that they wanted to kill large numbers of Americans.

The 9-11 commission concluded that the attacks occurred because terrorism was not an overriding national security concern before September 11, 2001. The commission said 9/11 was a terrible intelligence failure, although no single person was to blame.

"The United States government was simply not active enough in combating the terrorist threat before 9/11," Kean, a former governor of New Jersey, said when the 600-page report was released. Still, there's no way to know whether the attacks could have been prevented. "An attack of even greater magnitude is now possible and even probable. We do not have the luxury of time. We must prepare and we must act," Kean added.

After the attacks, the United States declared a "war on terror", and vowed to track down those responsible. Osama bin Laden was public enemy No. 1. Bin Laden, leader of the terrorist organization al-Qaeda, had been hiding in Afghanistan plotting the attacks along with several others, including Khalid Sheikh Mohammed. President Bush forged an international coalition to go after the terrorists. The United States and its allies began military operations in Afghanistan, which al-Qaeda used as its sanctuary.

AT A GLANCE

The clean up went on 24 hours a day, seven days a week. It took eight months to clear the site. Thousands of workers who worked long hours, helping to clear the debris, developed health issues.

W

Left: View of where the south tower of the world trade buildings stood.

Below: View of the Freedom Tower under construction at ground zero.

In America, the problems of 9/11 did not dissipate with time. Thousands of workers who worked long hours at ground zero fell ill. Nearly 70 percent began suffering from a variety of lung problems. Five years after the attacks, doctors at Mount Sinai Medical Center in New York concluded that the dust at Ground Zero had been toxic.

The Mount Sinai doctors examined 9,500 Ground Zero workers, including construction workers, police officers, firefighters, volunteers, and others. Doctors concluded that the rate of abnormal lung-function tests were double the general population. In 2010, Congress approved a $4.3 billion bill to cover the cost of medical care. Nearly 60,000 people enrolled in health-monitoring and treatment programs related to the 9/11 attack.

The collapse of the World Trade Center towers left a gaping hole in the city's skyline. Thousands had worked in the 110-story structures, while thousands of tourists visited each year to gaze out from the towers' observation deck.

But the World Trade Center was more than just an office building, or a tourist attraction. It was a symbol of human ingenuity and American financial might. The towers were once the tallest buildings in the world and an engineering marvel. Officials promised to fill the hole in New York's skyline with a bigger and better building.

In the summer of 2002, the group responsible for rebuilding announced a design competition for the new building. A number of different architectural, design, and engineering firms submitted plans for the site. In the end, officials selected a design by architect Daniel Libeskind. Libeskind's vision for the site underwent a series of changes.

Finally, on June 28, 2006, the public got its first glimpse of the new design. At the center of the project was a massive glass tower, originally named the Freedom Tower, but now named 1 World Trade Center Plaza. The new building will have 2.6 million square feet of office space, restaurants and an observation deck. The 104-story tower will stand 1,776 feet high. A 408-foot spire will rise from the top.

Upon its completion in 2013, the tower will be the tallest building in the United States. There will also be three other skyscrapers on the site. Each will surround The National September 11 Memorial & Museum dedicated to those who died and lived through the attacks.

Two of the original steel beams from the towers will be housed in the museum's glass entrance. The museum will tell the story of the dead, the survivors, and the rescue workers. Visitors will be able to see what is left of the "Survivor Stairs," the concrete steps that hundreds used to escape the destruction. The memorial will also contain the names of those who died.

On May 2, 2011, nearly 10 years after 9/11, the Americans killed the most wanted man in the world. Bin Laden was hiding in northern Pakistan, in a secluded walled-compound not far from a Pakistani military base. In the dead of night, U.S. Navy Seals stormed the compound and shot Osama bin Laden dead. The raid was the culmination of years of intelligence work by the United States.

Almost 3000 people died in the attacks. Many memorials exist in memory of those who died, and every year in New York City, on the anniversary, the names of the victims who died at the location are read out.

AT A GLANCE

The events of September 2001, were one of the most shocking of modern times, that rocked the United States to its very core. The images from its darkest day will forever be engrained in the minds of its citizens even as a new building rises from the ashes.

Above: Baronial coats of arms and royal seals surround the Magna Carta on this facsimile of the document.

Right: A painting showing King John signing the Magna Carta at Runnymede in 1215.

SIGNING OF THE MAGNA CARTA

RUNNYMEDE, ENGLAND
1215

The Magna Carta (Great Charter) is the most famous document ever produced, and was one of the most important in medieval Europe. It was drawn up to safeguard the rights of the nobility against the greedy King John, who kept raising taxes to fund his largely unsuccessful wars against France. However, more significantly, the charter also enshrined the rights of all free men of the realm: it promised them fair laws and access to legal courts without payment, and included the 'habeas corpus' clause, which meant no imprisonment without trial. In short it was the first ever bill of rights.

King John signed the charter, most reluctantly, at Runnymede, near Windsor Castle. He had been brought there by the barons who had united to take London and capture the king; they had considerable support from the people in carrying out this coup (and this favor would be repaid). Whilst the barons respected the king's right to govern, they were outraged not only by the massive feudal dues and taxes they had to pay, but also at the way he levied taxes – those who were out of favor could be saddled with a crippling tax debt whilst his favorites were excused. The wars in France were seen as just an opportunity for the monarchy to settle old scores and it was soon after another humiliating English defeat at Bouvines, France, that the nobles decided to come together.

There was mutual distrust at Runnymede, so there were clauses in the Magna Carta enabling the barons to enforce it through a council of 25. The barons knew that as soon as they disbanded their armies the king would assert his authority and destroy them, so they would not disarm. Their fears were probably justified. As soon as John got back to London he petitioned the Pope for permission to cancel his oath, which Rome soon granted.

King John's inability to act in good faith forced the barons to take the measures they did. Also, he badly overreached himself in his dealings with the nobility, and with the war in France. When it became obvious that the king was not going to abide by the charter, the barons had to choose whether to obey him or depose him. There was a split in their ranks. So there was general relief when, in October 1216, the king died. Ironically, subsequent rulers were more powerful than John, but the Magna Carta survived and was reissued in different forms. Even today some parts of it are legally valid, though the protection given by habeas corpus is now seen by many as being denied in the UK by the Prevention of Terrorism Act 2005.

AT A GLANCE

The Magna Carta was a charter drawn up by barons and agreed to by the English King John in 1215. One of its aims was to limit the king's power to levy taxes on the barons. But, more significantly, it also secured the liberty of all free men. Therefore it can be regarded as the original guarantee of human rights, inspiring the English, the Canadian and the US Bill of Rights.

COLUMBUS MAKES LANDFALL

THE BAHAMAS
OCTOBER 12, 1492

It was the Italian-born adventurer Cristoforo Colombo (known to the English-speaking world as Christopher Columbus) whose arrival in the New World kick-started the Spanish colonization of that continent. And while Columbus did not actually discover the Americas – that had already been done by the ancestors of the American natives, and by Vikings, Irish, Phoenicians and probably others from the eastern side of the Atlantic – it was his explorations that would be continued by other European countries, changing the continent forever. In the USA, the second Monday in October is still celebrated as Columbus Day.

Above: An artist's impression of Christopher Columbus making landfall in the New World.

Columbus was searching for a new trade route to the Indies, and was receiving financial support for his voyages from King Ferdinand and Queen Isabella of Spain. In the knowledge that the world was round, he suggested that a westward route from Europe to the Indies could be shorter and more direct than the perilous overland and coastal trade routes through what is now known as the Middle East. If true, this would give Spain control of the lucrative spice trade commanded until then by the Arabs and Italians.

In 1492 he set sail from Spain, taking his three ships, *Santa Maria*, *Pinta* and *Santa Clara* (later renamed *Niña*), to the Canary Islands to stock up on provisions. He made landfall in the Bahamas on October 12. Having underestimated the circumference of the Earth, he believed he had reached the Indies – hence the islands became known as the West Indies. His actual landing point remains the subject of discussion; the three most popular choices are Watling Island (San Salvador today), Cat Island, and Grand Turk.

He was motivated both by personal gain, having been promised his share of the riches – gold, pearls and spices – and by spreading Christianity, but his crew treated the local people, particularly the womenfolk, poorly. Furthermore, he lost the *Santa Maria*, the largest of the three ships entrusted to him, when it ran aground on Christmas Day and had to be abandoned.

Columbus returned to Europe without the promised treasure, but even so Ferdinand and Isabella gave him the title of Admiral of the Ocean Sea. He made three more voyages, the last in 1502, but never did manage to reach India and the Far East, his original goals. In fact, he never even reached the mainland of the American continent. He did, however, make it to Cuba (which he thought was China) and many other Caribbean islands. And when he died in 1506, two years after returning from his fourth voyage, he was still convinced that his journeys had been along the east coast of Asia.

AT A GLANCE

History credits Christopher Columbus with connecting the 15th-century Old World (Europe, Asia and Africa) to the New World (the Americas and the surrounding islands). The landfall he made on the first of his four voyages, in 1492, is still celebrated as Columbus Day in the United States.

Left: Replicas of the Pinta*, the* Santa Maria *and* Niña *set sail from Spain 500 years after Columbus.*

Above: A portrait of Ferdinand Magellan looking to the stars for navigational assistance.

MAGELLAN SETS SAIL FOR SOUTH AMERICA

SEVILLE, SPAIN
AUGUST 10, 1519

Portuguese-born sea captain Ferdinand Magellan set sail in August 1519 on the *Trinidad*, accompanied by four more ships. His intention, like that of Christopher Columbus before him, was to voyage to the Indies by sailing westward via the Americas rather than eastward as suggested by the prevailing land and coastal trade routes. Magellan, who had obtained Spanish nationality in order to serve Spain, also believed that the Pacific Ocean was much smaller than the Atlantic; according to the maps of the day, Japan was only a few hundred miles west of Mexico.

Magellan made initial landfall in Brazil, then sailed south in search of a river that he believed would take him through the continent to the ocean on its far side. But trial and error failed to locate any river. Eventually, in 1520, he discovered the narrow sea-passage now known as the Strait of Magellan, separating the southernmost tip of the South American continent from Tierra del Fuego. He was the first known European to reach that island.

He passed through the strait into the ocean which, due to its placid nature, he named the Pacific *(Tepre Pacificum*, 'peaceful sea'), and he sailed on for three months. But his crew suffered desperately, having to eat rats and drink polluted water to stay alive.

No land was sighted until in March 1521 Magellan reached the Philippines– but then on April 27, while attempting to convert the natives to Christianity, he was killed in the Battle of Mactan. It took 18 months for the expedition to sail on around Africa and return to Spain. By that time only 18 sailors were left alive of the original 250, and just one ship, the *Victoria*, out of the original five. But in September 1522, the surviving crew members had become the first known men to sail around the world, a journey that had taken three years.

Magellan's expedition had proved that Europeans could reach Asia by sailing west. But he failed in his quest to find a faster route to Asia from Spain, his route being much longer than the one around Africa. However, his voyage changed people's understanding of the Earth. The full size of the globe came to be understood, since the voyage was logged at 14,460 Spanish leagues – 60,440 km or 37,560 miles. The crew also found that despite having kept close watch on time, they turned out on their return to be a day behind, and so it was realized that what came to be known as the International Date Line would need to be established.

Right: A 17th-century map of the Strait of Magellan, the route from the Atlantic to the Pacific.

AT A GLANCE

Ferdinand Magellan's expedition from 1519 to 1522 was the first known to circumnavigate the world, even though he himself did not survive to return to Spain. He navigated the strait at the tip of South America, connecting the Atlantic and the Pacific Oceans, and he named it for himself.

Exquisita & magno aliquot mensium periculo lustrata et iam retecta Freti Magellanici Facies.
Eÿgentlicke afbeeldinghe der Magellanischer Strate die nu met veel gevaers ettelijke Maenden doorsien, van nieus ondecktis.
MAR
DEL
NORT
AME
RI
P
R
Het Derde Nau
Elisabeths Baij
Cabo Forward
Cabo d'Hollande
Mossel Baij
de quade Cordes Baij
Pinguijns Eijlanden
Het tweede Nau
t'Eerste Nau
Dese Eÿlanden die in gheene Pascaerten aengeteeckent bevonden en worden, Liggen van d'incomste der Strate Magellani O.N.O verscheijden 50 mijlen op de hoochde van 51 graden.

DEFEAT OF THE SPANISH ARMADA

ENGLISH CHANNEL/LA MANCHE

1588

The Armada, a 130-vessel naval force sent by Spain to invade England in July 1588, was repulsed by the British fleet, with the flamboyant Sir Francis Drake under the command of Lord Howard of Effingham. The Spanish plan had been that their ships would pick up soldiers in the Netherlands, then controlled by Spain, and ferry them across to England – but it was doomed to failure.

Three reasons lay behind Spain's action. First, its monopoly on trade in the Americas was being threatened by English privateers, and secondly its Catholic King Philip II wanted to reverse the Protestant ascendancy in England since Elizabeth had become queen; he saw this as a 'great evil'. Thirdly, England was helping the Dutch to resist Spanish rule, Protestantism being on the rise in the Netherlands, too.

The Armada, including 22 fighting galleons, sailed in a crescent shape to offer the cumbersome galleons maximum protection at the centre. As the Armada approached the coast of Cornwall on July 29, beacons were lit from hilltop to hilltop through the English countryside to warn the queen in London of its approach.

Sir Francis Drake is sometimes portrayed as showing admirable calm by finishing his game of bowls before setting sail, but the tide and wind were against him and he knew there was no point setting off till later; and when the British fleet did meet the Armada, its guns were ineffective against the massive timbers of the galleons. But when the Spanish dropped anchor off Calais to await overnight for the arrival of their troops from the Netherlands, Drake set light to a number of fireships, which drifted into the Spaniards' midst.

The Armada scattered in panic, and so the Spanish galleons were more vulnerable to British gunfire. Worse, bad weather made it impossible for them to follow their favored style of naval battle, firing broadsides at the enemy ships before boarding them. Three of their galleons were sunk, with 600 men killed and 800 wounded; the rest found their escape route back down the Channel blocked by headwinds and the English, and were forced to sail up the east coast of England and round Scotland to return home.

Just over 60 ships out of the original force of 130 returned to Spain – half the fleet had been sunk or wrecked. Over 20,000 Spanish sailors and soldiers were killed, whereas the English, throughout the whole campaign, lost no ships and only 100 men in battle. However, over 7,000 English sailors died from disease, mostly dysentery and typhus, while the Armada remained in English waters. Defeated King Philip II of Spain blamed the Armada's failure on the weather, saying, "I sent you out to war with men, not with the wind and waves." Whatever the truth, Sir Francis Drake's reputation was immeasurably enhanced, while Spain's reputation as a world power was significantly damaged.

Above: Sir Francis Drake completes his game of bowls on Plymouth Hoe before setting sail.

Left: The Spanish Armada advances up the English Channel to meet its fate.

AT A GLANCE

The Armada was sent by Philip II of Spain in the summer of 1588 to invade England. The Armada's defeat signaled the decline of Spain as a great European power, as well as the end of the Spanish trade monopoly in North America and Asia. English sea dog Sir Francis Drake became a folk hero, reputed to have finished his game of bowls before routing the foe.

INVENTION OF THE SPINNING JENNY

LEIGH, LANCASHIRE, ENGLAND
1764

Above: An illustration depicting James Hargreaves' Spinning Jenny.

Left: A woman working in an automated cotton mill in the early 20th century.

The invention of the Spinning Jenny was the single most important event of the early industrial revolution. It introduced mass production to the spinning of cotton, a vital stage in the process of making cloth. This mechanization began the transformation of cloth production from a cottage industry to factory production in the 'dark satanic mills' of industrial England.

As with so many important innovations, several men laid claim to it, and other men's innovations certainly paved the way for it. In 1733 John Kay patented a flying shuttle, which allowed a weaver to make cloth wider than the reach of his outstretched arm. In 1760, his son Robert devised the drop box, a way of making patterns by using three colors of weft (the woven, horizontal thread) on a single loom. Wider cloth and multiple yarns meant that weavers needed more thread; the first Spinning Jenny allowed one spinner to run six spindles at a time, instead of the previous single spindle.

Its invention is generally credited to Thomas Highs of Leigh in 1764, although the idea was more fully developed three years later by James Hargreaves in Blackburn. Hargreaves' new machines were destroyed by rioting spinners who feared that they would be put out of work. They were right of course; ten years later, there were 20,000 Spinning Jennies operating in Britain.

Hargreaves fled to Nottingham, arriving there at about the same time as Richard Arkwright, an entrepreneur who further developed the Spinning Jenny by using water power. Arkwright opened his first water-powered mill at Cromford in Derbyshire, and eventually had a chain of Arkwright mills from Lancashire to Lanarkshire in Scotland. He too faced resistance to his innovations when protesters burnt down his mill at Birkacre in Lancashire in 1779.

That year, Samuel Crompton combined the ideas of Arkwright, Hargreaves and Highs in the Spinning Mule, a machine capable of producing finer thread than its predecessors. Further innovations followed, leap-frogging one another in the race to increase output and improve quality. In 1785 a steam engine by James Watt was used to power a cotton mill for the first time, and the Rev Edmund Cartwright patented a power loom.

Cartwright looms were the target for arsonists in Manchester in 1792. But the rioters and arsonists couldn't stop progress; the technology was applied to other industries. In due course mechanization transformed not only manufacturing processes but the structure and politics of British society. It changed the very landscape of Britain, too, which became dotted and crossed by mills and factories, canals and railways, and new towns and cities.

AT A GLANCE

The invention of the Spinning Jenny was representative of the industrial revolution, by which mechanization replaced hand-driven skills and enabled greater profits to be made by manufacturers and mill owners. Resistance from the working classes was inevitable, but ultimately futile.

COOK SETS SAIL FOR THE PACIFIC

PLYMOUTH, ENGLAND
1768

Explorer and cartographer Lieutenant James Cook set sail from Plymouth in his converted coal-carrier, the *Endeavour*, in 1768, bound for the Pacific. He had been ordered by the Royal Society to observe Venus passing in front of the sun, an event that could be used to help measure the distance from the sun to the Earth.

Cook reached New Zealand, which had previously been discovered by the Dutchman Abel Tasman, in 1770; Cook circumnavigated and charted both north and south islands before continuing westwards. When he reached the east coast of New Holland (later to be known as Australia), he named his anchorage Botany Bay, and the land itself New South Wales; on 26 August, he claimed it for Britain and King George III. Then he sailed northwards, on a four-month voyage along the eastern coast of the continent.

In 1788 the British Captain Arthur Phillip followed Cook, to find a perfect natural harbour which he named after Britain's then Home Secretary, Lord Sydney, and the British started settling the continent, mainly through the transportation of British convicts.

Cook was the first person to accurately chart a large part of the Australian coastline, his 12 years sailing around the Pacific Ocean contributing much to European knowledge of the area. On his second voyage, on *Resolution*, he managed to determine longitude with higher accuracy than anyone had achieved before, using the newfangled chronometer and a Gregory Azimuth Compass. He also understood how important it was to eat vegetables to reduce scurvy, the sometimes fatal illness that resulted from dietary deficiency on long voyages. He succeeded in completing his first voyage without losing a single man to the disease.

Cook is ranked with Vasco de Gama and Columbus among explorers, and is considered a major figure in Australia's modern history. Many places, both on the east Australian coast and in New Zealand, have been named after him or the *Endeavour*, and many of the names he gave to places in 1770, such as Botany Bay and the Whitsundays in the Great Barrier Reef, are still used today. He died on an expedition to Hawaii in 1779, his third voyage of discovery, and is commemorated by a statue in Greenwich, London, UK.

AT A GLANCE

In 1770, Lieutenant (later Captain) James Cook was the man who discovered Australia. He was an innovator in the process of long-distance sea travel and navigation, reaching six of the seven continents during his lifetime, and is rightly remembered as one of the foremost explorers of his era.

Left: Landfall at Botany Bay.

Inset: Captain Cook's orders to discover Australia, on display in the Public Records Office, London.

IN CONGRESS, JULY 4, 1776.

The unanimous Declaration of the thirteen united States of America,

When in the Course of human events, it becomes necessary for one people to dissolve the political bands which have connected them with another, and to assume among the powers of the earth, the separate and equal station to which the Laws of Nature and of Nature's God entitle them, a decent respect to the opinions of mankind requires that they should declare the causes which impel them to the separation. —— We hold these truths to be self-evident, that all men are created equal, that they are endowed by their Creator with certain unalienable Rights, that among these are Life, Liberty and the pursuit of Happiness. — That to secure these rights, Governments are instituted among Men, deriving their just powers from the consent of the governed, — That whenever any Form of Government becomes destructive of these ends, it is the Right of the People to alter or to abolish it, and to institute new Government, laying its foundation on such principles and organizing its powers in such form, as to them shall seem most likely to effect their Safety and Happiness. Prudence, indeed, will dictate that Governments long established should not be changed for light and transient causes; and accordingly all experience hath shewn, that mankind are more disposed to suffer, while evils are sufferable, than to right themselves by abolishing the forms to which they are accustomed. But when a long train of abuses and usurpations, pursuing invariably the same Object evinces a design to reduce them under absolute Despotism, it is their right, it is their duty, to throw off such Government, and to provide new Guards for their future security. — Such has been the patient sufferance of these Colonies; and such is now the necessity which constrains them to alter their former Systems of Government. The history of the present King of Great Britain is a history of repeated injuries and usurpations, all having in direct object the establishment of an absolute Tyranny over these States. To prove this, let Facts be submitted to a candid world. —— He has refused his Assent to Laws, the most wholesome and necessary for the public good. —— He has forbidden his Governors to pass Laws of immediate and pressing importance, unless suspended in their operation till his Assent should be obtained; and when so suspended, he has utterly neglected to attend to them. —— He has refused to pass other Laws for the accommodation of large districts of people, unless those people would relinquish the right of Representation in the Legislature, a right inestimable to them and formidable to tyrants only. —— He has called together legislative bodies at places unusual, uncomfortable, and distant from the depository of their public Records, for the sole purpose of fatiguing them into compliance with his measures. —— He has dissolved Representative Houses repeatedly, for opposing with manly firmness his invasions on the rights of the people. —— He has refused for a long time, after such dissolutions, to cause others to be elected; whereby the Legislative powers, incapable of Annihilation, have returned to the People at large for their exercise; the State remaining in the mean time exposed to all the dangers of invasion from without, and convulsions within. —— He has endeavoured to prevent the population of these States; for that purpose obstructing the Laws for Naturalization of Foreigners; refusing to pass others to encourage their migrations hither, and raising the conditions of new Appropriations of Lands. —— He has obstructed the Administration of Justice, by refusing his Assent to Laws for establishing Judiciary powers. —— He has made Judges dependent on his Will alone, for the tenure of their offices, and the amount and payment of their salaries. —— He has erected a multitude of New Offices, and sent hither swarms of Officers to harrass our people, and eat out their substance. —— He has kept among us, in times of peace, Standing Armies without the Consent of our legislatures. —— He has affected to render the Military independent of and superior to the Civil power. —— He has combined with others to subject us to a jurisdiction foreign to our constitution, and unacknowledged by our laws; giving his Assent to their Acts of pretended Legislation: — For Quartering large bodies of armed troops among us: — For protecting them, by a mock Trial, from punishment for any Murders which they should commit on the Inhabitants of these States: — For cutting off our Trade with all parts of the world: — For imposing Taxes on us without our Consent: — For depriving us in many cases, of the benefits of Trial by Jury: — For transporting us beyond Seas to be tried for pretended offences: — For abolishing the free System of English Laws in a neighbouring Province, establishing therein an Arbitrary government, and enlarging its Boundaries so as to render it at once an example and fit instrument for introducing the same absolute rule into these Colonies: — For taking away our Charters, abolishing our most valuable Laws, and altering fundamentally the Forms of our Governments: — For suspending our own Legislatures, and declaring themselves invested with power to legislate for us in all cases whatsoever. — He has abdicated Government here, by declaring us out of his Protection and waging War against us. —— He has plundered our seas, ravaged our Coasts, burnt our towns, and destroyed the lives of our people. —— He is at this time transporting large Armies of foreign Mercenaries to compleat the works of death, desolation and tyranny, already begun with circumstances of Cruelty & perfidy scarcely paralleled in the most barbarous ages, and totally unworthy the Head of a civilized nation. —— He has constrained our fellow Citizens taken Captive on the high Seas to bear Arms against their Country, to become the executioners of their friends and Brethren, or to fall themselves by their Hands. —— He has excited domestic insurrections amongst us, and has endeavoured to bring on the inhabitants of our frontiers, the merciless Indian Savages, whose known rule of warfare, is an undistinguished destruction of all ages, sexes and conditions. In every stage of these Oppressions We have Petitioned for Redress in the most humble terms: Our repeated Petitions have been answered only by repeated injury. A Prince, whose character is thus marked by every act which may define a Tyrant, is unfit to be the ruler of a free people. Nor have We been wanting in attentions to our Brittish brethren. We have warned them from time to time of attempts by their legislature to extend an unwarrantable jurisdiction over us. We have reminded them of the circumstances of our emigration and settlement here. We have appealed to their native justice and magnanimity, and we have conjured them by the ties of our common kindred to disavow these usurpations, which, would inevitably interrupt our connections and correspondence. They too have been deaf to the voice of justice and of consanguinity. We must, therefore, acquiesce in the necessity, which denounces our Separation, and hold them, as we hold the rest of mankind, Enemies in War, in Peace Friends. ——

We, therefore, the Representatives of the united States of America, in General Congress, Assembled, appealing to the Supreme Judge of the world for the rectitude of our intentions, do, in the Name, and by Authority of the good People of these Colonies, solemnly publish and declare, That these United Colonies are, and of Right ought to be Free and Independent States; that they are Absolved from all Allegiance to the British Crown, and that all political connection between them and the State of Great Britain, is and ought to be totally dissolved; and that as Free and Independent States, they have full Power to levy War, conclude Peace, contract Alliances, establish Commerce, and to do all other Acts and Things which Independent States may of right do. —— And for the support of this Declaration, with a firm reliance on the protection of divine Providence, we mutually pledge to each other our Lives, our Fortunes and our sacred Honor.

John Hancock

Button Gwinnett
Lyman Hall
Geo Walton

Wm Hooper
Joseph Hewes
John Penn

Edward Rutledge
Thos Heyward Junr.
Thomas Lynch Junr.
Arthur Middleton

Samuel Chase
Wm Paca
Thos Stone
Charles Carroll of Carrollton

George Wythe
Richard Henry Lee
Th Jefferson
Benja Harrison

Robt Morris
Benjamin Rush
Benja Franklin
John Morton
Geo Clymer
Jas Smith
Geo Taylor
James Wilson
Geo Ross
Caesar Rodney
Geo Read
Tho M:Kean

Wm Floyd
Phil Livingston
Frans Lewis
Lewis Morris
Richd Stockton
Jno Witherspoon
Fras Hopkinson
John Hart
Abra Clark

Josiah Bartlett
Wm Whipple
Saml Adams
John Adams
Robt Treat Paine
Elbridge Gerry
Step Hopkins
William Ellery
Roger Sherman
Sam el Huntington
Wm Williams
Oliver Wolcott

Above: The Assembly Room in Philadelphia where the Declaration was signed.

Left: The historic Declaration of Independence.

Overleaf: John Trumbull's Declaration of Independence depicting the presentation of the draft of the Declaration of Independence to Congress.

US DECLARATION OF INDEPENDENCE

PHILADELPHIA, USA

JULY 4, 1776

The birth of the United States of America in 1776 was the result of a struggle against British rule by her American colonies. The British government had run up debts in wars against France and India, and so had decided to increase taxation. But the British living in America resented this, especially because they had no say in the decisions made by the British parliament; their slogan 'No taxation without representation' summed up what they felt.

In September 1774, representatives of twelve of the self-governing provinces convened in Philadelphia, forming the First Continental Congress, in an attempt to coordinate a response to Britain's demands. But when their negotiations – and even their petition to King George III to intervene – proved fruitless, they decided to boycott British goods and services.

The citizens of Boston tipped British tea into their harbor as a protest against the taxation on tea and sugar, and many colonists refused to pay the stamp duty levied on documents. In 1775, colonist Patrick Henry expressed the feelings of many who until this time had considered themselves British subjects: he called for his fellows to place their loyalties to one side and put their lives on the line in the pursuit of liberty.

In 1776 the British Parliament passed the Prohibitory Act, creating a blockade of American ports and declaring American ships to be enemy vessels. This strengthened public support in the colonies, and John Adams, a keen supporter of independence, said that by doing this, Parliament had declared American independence before Congress had been able to do it.

On July 4, 1776, 55 men, representing the 13 colonies, each put their signature to the Declaration of Independence, drafted principally by Thomas Jefferson; it claimed sovereignty for the territories and rejected their allegiance to Britain. About 200 copies were printed and circulated throughout the colonies for public reading. The original document signed by Congress is now preserved in the National Archives, though several early copies also exist.

The War of Independence had actually already begun a year earlier, with skirmishes at Lexington and Concord in which about 55 men had died. The war continued, with France helping the colonists, until it was officially ended by the 1783 Treaty of Paris. This recognized the sovereignty of the USA over land reaching from Canada to the north to Florida to the south and to the Mississippi to the west. The Constitution of the United States followed five years later.

The signing of the Declaration is celebrated in the USA every July 4, Independence Day.

AT A GLANCE

In 1776, 13 colonies in North America united to sign Thomas Jefferson's Declaration of Independence, breaking free of the British Empire and becoming the United States of America. The new nation, founded principally because the colonists rejected the idea of being taxed without parliamentary representation, is now considered by many as the leader of the free world.

Above: King Louis XVI, whose execution followed four years later, in 1793.

Right: A contemporary illustration of the Fall of the Bastille by artist Jean-Pierre Houel.

FALL OF THE BASTILLE

PARIS, FRANCE
JULY 14, 1789

By 1787, it had become impossible to govern France effectively. Inflation was rampant, the state was impoverished by long wars, and outdated farming practices and ancient feudal systems combined to keep the peasants poor and hungry. Ministers of the king, Louis XVI, tried to carry out political reforms that year, but the aristocracy, who saw the proposed reforms as a threat to their status, thwarted them at every turn.

In May 1789, under pressure from both his government and the population as a whole, the king reluctantly gave the French people a role in government for the first time in history. The new National Constituent Assembly met for the first time on July 9 – but just two days later, the nobles persuaded the king to sack his finance minister, who had supported the reforms.

News of his dismissal spread rapidly through Paris. The people, believing that this was the start of a counter-attack by the old regime, protested by raiding tax offices and food depots. Skirmishes broke out as weapons and wheat were 'liberated'. On the morning of July 14, the angry demonstrators seized a hoard of 30,000 firearms, and began a hunt for gunpowder and shot.

The Bastille was an old fortress, so badly designed that it had been captured at every one of the six sieges in its 400-year history. As a prison it had already been slated for closure before the riots broke out; on the day it was stormed, it held only seven inmates. But the space left unoccupied by prisoners housed a huge arsenal of explosives, and it was for this that the rabble raided the building.

The frenzied crowd quickly overcame the inadequate defense force. Bloodthirsty after three days of rioting, the mob brutally murdered the prison governor and began an orgy of drunken celebration in the Paris streets – contemporary reports say that many of them dropped dead from sheer exhaustion. But the victorious revolutionaries somehow found the energy to demolish the building almost immediately, stone by stone. All that remain today are a few foundations, visible in the Bastille metro station, and some masonry re-used in the bridge over the Seine at the Place de la Concorde.

The importance of the Bastille as a prison and a garrison may have been exaggerated in the centuries since its overthrow, but its strength as a symbol of the violent destruction of the old order is undeniable. The French Revolution launched 60 years of political upheaval that would transform the social structure of Europe. *Quatorze juillet* 1789 was the beginning of the end of feudalism in France – it was the day that for the first time its ordinary people took control of their destiny.

AT A GLANCE

The demolition of the Bastille prison in Paris in July 1789 signaled the beginning of the French Revolution, as the downtrodden people rose up against King Louis XVI and the aristocracy that had kept them subjugated. Today, France, now a republic, still celebrates 'le quatorze juillet' every year.

BATTLE OF WATERLOO

BELGIUM
JUNE 18, 1815

For 18 years Napoleon Bonaparte, in expanding his empire, had brought war to much of Europe, and this had turned many of its countries into enemies of France. These countries formed a coalition, and in 1814 Paris fell to their invading forces. Bonaparte was captured by them and sent into exile on the island of Elba, but he was held for less than a year; in February 1815 he escaped and rode up through France to Paris. There, he was hailed as emperor once again by the French people, and large parts of the French Army decided to serve under him.

Britain, Russia, Prussia and Austria formed an alliance to crush Napoleon once and for all. They each pledged 150,000 men for an invasion of France, which was planned for July 1. Napoleon, however – brilliant general as he was – seized the initiative, deciding to attack the individual enemy armies before they had a chance to combine forces against him.

He boldly invaded Belgium, and on June 16 his French army fought on two fronts, defeating Field Marshal Blücher's Prussian army at Ligny, and managing to stall the British army under the Duke of Wellington at Quatre Bras. Wellington's troops withdrew to the village of Waterloo, while the Prussians regrouped further east.

At Waterloo on the morning of June 18, battle recommenced. The French infantry advanced first, but were repulsed by British firepower and cavalry. Next, a French cavalry counterattack wreaked heavy losses on the British cavalry. But then the British infantry redcoats formed tight squares and advanced, and the French cavalry, despite repeated charges, were unable to penetrate them; the fearsome rapid fire of the British musketeers decimated the French.

The French managed, however, to capture La Haye farmhouse, a strategic position which their artillery used to launch a devastating bombardment onto the British squares. Napoleon sent in his crack troops, the Imperial Guard, to cut a path through the British forces and take on the Prussian army, now arriving on the field.

But for the first time in their history the Imperial Guard were defeated; it was the British guardsmen and light infantry who together achieved this. As the news of the Guard's disgrace spread, French morale collapsed – and Wellington chose this moment to signal a general advance. The French army fled, pursued and brutally cut down by the Prussian cavalry, vengeful from their defeat the day before.

Bonaparte was broken. His support in Paris melted away, and he fled the city, hoping to sail to America. But the Royal Navy had blockaded the ports, and less than two weeks later, Napoleon surrendered to a British sea captain. He was imprisoned this time on the remote island of St Helena, where he died in exile in 1821. France's power in Europe was broken, and Britain did not fight another major war for 100 years.

Above: Napoleon's defeat at Waterloo preceded his exile to the island of Elba.

Left: An illustration from the painting by H Chartier depicting the Battle of Waterloo.

AT A GLANCE

Napoleon was defeated at Waterloo in 1815 by allied armies under Wellington from Britain and Blücher from Prussia. The defeat not only broke the French emperor's will and health but also his country's stranglehold over Europe, changing the face of the continent. He was sent into exile and he died six years later.

Above: Trains pass each other on the Liverpool and Manchester Railway, in an illustration by Clavell.

Right: The Northumbrian, *the first locomotive on the Liverpool and Manchester Railway, pictured during centennial celebrations in 1930.*

OPENING OF THE LIVERPOOL–MANCHESTER RAILWAY

UK
SEPTEMBER 15, 1830

The Liverpool and Manchester Railway Company (L&MR) was formed in 1823, and three years later the British parliament allowed it to construct the first public passenger railway line in the world. The route was a challenge for its engineer, George Stephenson, as in its 32 miles the line had to cross wide valleys, cut through stone hillsides and even in one section be floated across an apparently bottomless peat bog.

When the line was nearly completed, a competition of speed, strength and endurance was held on a test track at Rainhill, to find the best engine to run between the two cities. The winner was Stephenson's locomotive *Rocket*. But between the trial and the opening of the line Stephenson improved his design, and as a result it was another of his locomotives, the *Northumbrian*, which hauled the coaches full of eminent guests on the inaugural run on September 15, 1830.

The line was a double track, and the plan was for the *Northumbrian's* train to pause at a certain point to allow the dignitaries on board to view a procession of locomotives travelling on the other track. Some of the guests took advantage of the stop to get out and stretch their legs – and joy turned to horror at the first death on a passenger railway, when a member of parliament fell while attempting to get out of the way of the oncoming cavalcade. His legs were crushed under the *Rocket's* wheels, and he died soon afterwards.

Despite that discouraging event, the opening of the Liverpool and Manchester Railway made a phenomenal impact. Its immediate success – and the profits it made – prompted the railway mania of the 1830s and 1840s; by the end of those two decades, there were over 5,000 miles of railway in Britain, transforming the landscape.

The speed, convenience and comfort of rail travel hastened the end of long-distance coaches and horses. In fact, passenger traffic on the nation's roads never really grew until the car was invented. The rail freight service outshone the canal system, which could not compete with the speed at which the railway could carry perishable goods and urgent mail. This meant that the trains took over the transport of raw materials and products to and from the industrial heartlands.

Those heartlands went on to supply railways to the world, using the track gauge and other innovations introduced by Stephenson for the L&MR. The 19th century became known as the Railway Age, and Stephenson as the Father of the Railways.

AT A GLANCE

The opening of a 32-mile track between the northern British industrial centres of Liverpool and Manchester confirmed the railway as the coming mode of transport for both passengers and freight, ending the era of horse and coach. Rail would rule until the rise of motor transport in the next century.

NORTHUMBRIAN

PARLIAMENT PASSES THE EMANCIPATION ACT

LONDON, UK
JULY 26, 1833

The Emancipation Act in 1833 put the finishing touch to a gradual shift in social attitudes that had begun nearly 50 years earlier. Back in 1787, the Society for the Abolition of Slavery had been founded by Quakers, and that same year the British Prime Minister, William Pitt the Younger, had asked a young MP, William Wilberforce, to lead the abolition movement in parliament.

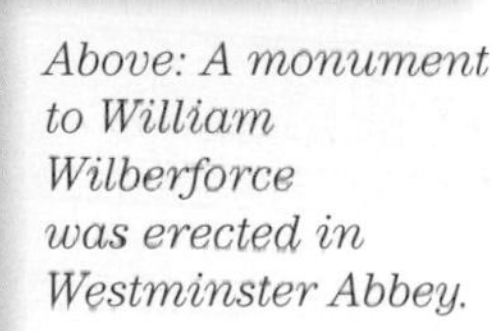

Above: A monument to William Wilberforce was erected in Westminster Abbey.

Left: A contemporary illustration of an anti-slavery public meeting held in Exeter Hall, London.

Wilberforce was an evangelical Christian, and it was these Non-Conformists and Dissenters who so strongly supported humanitarian progress. But the Church of England, the state religion, was at best indifferent, some of its clergymen even owning slaves themselves.

As the years went by, the British people became more and more opposed to the cruel injustices of the slave trade, but political and vested interests blocked every attempt to pass laws to restrict it. Although Wilberforce presented an abolition bill in Parliament almost every year from 1789 onwards, he had to wait for nearly 20 years, when in 1807 a new government was in power, for his bill to be passed.

It was an important first step, because it outlawed the trade in slaves carried out by British ships. But trade by other countries, particularly Portugal, continued – and in any case it was still legal to own slaves, as against transporting them. So Wilberforce was adamant that slavery itself must be ended, and he continued to campaign.

In 1823 a new Anti-Slavery Society was formed, and Wilberforce published a pamphlet that made his points with his usual verve and vigor. But the years of fighting and frustration had worn him down, and he began to take a less active role. He retired from Parliament in 1825, and in 1830 he chaired the Anti-Slavery Society for the last time. But by then the tide had turned, and the political will which Wilberforce had worked for so long to influence was at last reflecting the people's support for the cause.

At last, on July 26, 1833, the Abolition of Slavery Act had its final reading in the House of Commons, to become law on August 1 the following year. There were still compromises – slaves were to be reclassified as 'tied apprentices' for up to six years, and the government had to pay out over £20 million in compensation to the planters who had bought them. But it was the beginning of the end for a great inhumanity, and a sinking William Wilberforce was able to say, "Thank God that I have lived to witness a day in which England is willing to give twenty millions sterling for the abolition of slavery." He died just three days later, on July 29, 1833.

AT A GLANCE

The long, hard battle against slavery cost politician William Wilberforce his health and ultimately his life. But the Emancipation Act passed in 1833 gave thousands upon thousands of people their lives back, as the other politicians finally gave in to half a century of public opinion, and the vested interests of the ruling classes were overcome.

Above: The south transept of the Crystal Palace, built for the Great Exhibition of 1851, being reconstructed in Sydenham.

Right: A contemporary engraving of the Great Exhibition, Main Avenue, looking east.

Overleaf: A contemporary engraving of the South Transept of the Crystal Palace.

THE GREAT EXHIBITION OPENS

LONDON, UK
MAY 1, 1851

By the mid-19th century Britain was at peace with itself and the world. It had not fought a war since defeating the French at Waterloo. It had survived political upheavals at home and abroad, including the chaotic year of 1848 when so many European nations had suffered armed revolt. And now, thanks to its own industrial revolution, Britain was experiencing an explosion of wealth.

It was Prince Albert, Queen Victoria's German husband, who had come up with the idea of a Great Exhibition. He had overcome early unpopularity by throwing himself into British life; he reinvented the Royal Family as role model for the nation's nuclear families, and he took a great interest in national politics.

Albert was a modern man, an admirer of innovation and the application of science. He was made President of the Royal Society for the Encouragement of Arts, Manufacture and Commerce in 1843 and, seeing the Society's annual exhibitions and the French Industrial Exposition of 1844, was inspired by the idea of staging an international festival of industrial design in Britain.

Although the Exhibition was to include almost as many overseas exhibits as British ones, the main idea was to show off the achievements of Britain and its Empire by comparison with the rest of the world. The very building in which it was housed, the Crystal Palace, was a marvel of engineering and modular mass production. It was longer than the French royal palace at Versailles and taller than Westminster Abbey, and its one million square feet of glass easily enclosed a number of full-size trees that were growing on the site in Hyde Park, in the heart of London.

In this way, Britain demonstrated to the world its belief in its mastery over nature and science. The Exhibition gave the British a sense of superiority, security and confidence which helped keep their morale high for the next hundred years. But the Exhibition also acted as a forum for the international exchange of ideas; some of the exhibits from overseas producers, including Britain's industrial successors, the USA and Germany, inspired a new wave of simpler design and more efficient mass production.

The Crystal Palace was dismantled after the exhibition and rebuilt in south London, where in 1911, as the home of the Festival of Empire, it briefly relived its former glory. It burned down in 1936.

The Great Exhibition was visited by six million people between May and October 1851, and was a fabulous money-spinner. The profits – £186,000, or over £16 million ($24 million) in today's money – were used to found the Science Museum, the Natural History Museum, and the Victoria and Albert Museum in neighboring Kensington.

AT A GLANCE

Britain's Great Exhibition of 1851 was the brainchild of Queen Victoria's husband, Prince Albert, and it was intended to publicize Britain's achievements. It more than met its aims, inspiring designers from many countries worldwide, while its profits funded three major museums that still inform and enlighten to this day.

BRITISH
TO THE GALLERIES.

PERRY BOMBARDS TOKYO – JAPAN OPENS UP TO THE MODERN WORLD

TOKYO, JAPAN
JULY 8, 1853

Above: Commodore Matthew Perry meets the Japanese royal commissioner at Yokohama.

Left: US naval forces sail into Tokyo harbour.

In the mid-19th century, Japanese ports were closed to foreigners, apart from a handful of Dutch and Chinese traders at Nagasaki. Japan's rulers, the feudal Tokugawa shogunate, resisted contact with outsiders, both commercial and diplomatic. The USA and other nations had tried to open channels of communication, but had been consistently rebuffed. Then in 1849, after Captain James Glynn had secured the release of some American sailors imprisoned in Nagasaki, he recommended to the US Congress that the United States should send in a diplomatic mission – backed up, if they felt it necessary, by force.

For the US government it was vital to gain access to Japanese ports, in order to restock its commercial whaling fleet with coal and other supplies, and the prospect of trading with Japan was a bonus. So in 1852, US President Millard Fillmore ordered Commodore Matthew C. Perry to sail the US Navy's East India Squadron to Japan, to establish diplomatic relations.

Perry had had a distinguished naval career. In 1822, he had taken the Caribbean island of Key West for the USA. During the Mexican–American War, he had been appointed Commander of the Navy's Home Squadron, and he had personally led the attack on Tabasco, in central Mexico, in 1847. Having modernized the US fleet, he was known as the 'Father of the Steam Navy'.

Four black vessels arrived in Tokyo Harbor on July 8, 1853, causing amazement amongst the native population, who had not seen steamships before. The Japanese told Perry to carry on to Nagasaki, but he refused and ordered his ships, with their powerful Paixhans shell guns, to bombard Tokyo harbor. The Japanese, realizing that they could not defend themselves against such might, allowed Perry to deliver a formal request from the US President for a treaty.

In February 1854, Perry returned to Japan, and was given a document which agreed to most of the United States' demands. This became the Convention of Kanagawa, or the America–Japan Treaty of Amity and Friendship. It led to commercial trade between the United States and Japan, and also contributed to opening up of Japan to other Western nations, with the resulting blending of cultures.

This hastened the downfall of the Tokugawa shogunate and the modernization of the Japanese state. Commodore Perry, meanwhile, received a grant of $20,000 from the US Congress as a reward for his work in opening up trade relations between Japan and the rest of the world.

AT A GLANCE

A blunt display of naval might by the United States in 1853 helped break down the barriers that the proudly insular Japanese rulers had put up against the Western world. The agreement that resulted from this demonstration helped change the form of government in Japan, made trade easier, and opened up lines of communication between Japan and the Western world that would last for nearly a century.

DARWIN'S ORIGIN OF SPECIES PUBLISHED

LONDON, UK
NOVEMBER 24, 1859

ON

THE ORIGIN OF SPECIES

BY MEANS OF NATURAL SELECTION,

OR THE

PRESERVATION OF FAVOURED RACES IN THE STRUGGLE FOR LIFE.

BY CHARLES DARWIN, M.A.,

FELLOW OF THE ROYAL, GEOLOGICAL, LINNÆAN, ETC., SOCIETIES;
AUTHOR OF 'JOURNAL OF RESEARCHES DURING H. M. S. BEAGLE'S VOYAGE ROUND THE WORLD.'

LONDON:
JOHN MURRAY, ALBEMARLE STREET.
1859.

The right of Translation is reserved.

Above: The title page of Charles Darwin's revolutionary book, On the Origin of Species, *published in 1859.*

Right: An 1875 photograph of naturalist Charles Darwin.

AT A GLANCE

Medical student Charles Darwin's enquiring mind encouraged him to look beyond the Biblical explanation of Earth's creation and to suggest an alternative means of evolution. His On the Origin of Species *became a standard text in spite of vehement religious opposition.*

The young Charles Darwin had taken a keen interest in natural history, or 'natural theology' as it was known. According to prevailing wisdom, God had created a fixed order of natural life, and any variations in it were according to God's laws. But Darwin was aware of new theories of evolution which were beginning to challenge that entrenched Christian view.

As a medical student in Edinburgh, he had spent more time studying marine invertebrates than attending surgery demonstrations, which he found upsetting. It was, however, as a geologist that he joined the survey ship HMS *Beagle* in 1831 on its second voyage around the world. During that five-year journey he studied fossil records as well as plant and animal life.

His observations, including those of the differing species of finches found on the islands of the Galapagos group, suggested to him the notion of natural selection. He reasoned that a sequence of variations in a given species could over time lead to the evolution of a new species, if those variations were favorable for the survival in a particular habitat.

It was survival of the fittest This realization implied that the natural order was not fixed by God; it could change – indeed had changed – in response to circumstances. It was a theory which directly contradicted the accepted ideas of natural theology, and Darwin proceeded with caution, aware of the hostility his views might arouse.

While he conducted more research and built his reputation as a biologist, other scientists were independently converging on his ideas. In 1844, an anonymous publication, *Vestiges of the Natural History of Creation*, contained a crude version of evolutionary theory and provoked the fury of the clergy, but spurred Darwin and others to greater fieldwork and study.

A paper delivered in 1855 by one of those other scientists, Alfred Russel Wallace, convinced Darwin of the need to get into print with his ideas, and so *On the Origin of Species by Means of Natural Selection, or the Preservation of Favoured Races in the Struggle for Life* finally appeared, more than 20 years after the voyage of the *Beagle*. To avoid controversy, his text actually made no reference at all to the evolution of human beings – nevertheless he still faced the angry condemnation of those opposed to the idea of mankind being 'descended from the apes'.

The concept of evolution was quickly adopted by the scientific community, but only in the 1930s was Darwin's theory of natural selection fully accepted. It is now the cornerstone of the life sciences, although the recent resurgence of fundamentalist Christianity has created new opposition to it.

Above: *Richard Gatling received patents for drills, toilets and tractors, but is best remembered for the Gatling gun.*

Right: *The patent diagram for the Gatling gun, the world's first practical multiple-barrel machine gun.*

Below: *US soldiers use a Gatling gun during the Philippine Insurrection in 1899.*

INVENTION OF THE GATLING GUN

USA
1861

The Gatling gun won its place in military history for being the world's first rapid-fire weapon that by means of mechanical rotation of barrels could shoot more quickly than any hand-cocked weapon. The sustained bursts it delivered could amount to 200 rounds per minute – an amazing rate of fire for its time. It was effectively one of the first machine guns.

When Dr Richard Gatling invented the gun in 1861 during the American Civil War, he expressed the rather naïve belief that the gun's potential to kill and maim would make future soldiers think twice before engaging in battle. Failing that, it would reduce the numbers of soldiers needed to risk their lives on the battlefield.

It was first used by the Union in the Civil War in its victory over the Confederates, but was so radical in design that Gatling was unable to persuade the government to buy it. But Major General Benjamin F. Butler privately purchased 12 guns for $1,000 each, to be used on the Petersburg front in 1864.

The original Gatling had revolving barrels needing manual cranking, and so it ceded the honor of being the first true fully automatic weapon to the Maxim gun, invented by the American-born British inventor Sir Hiram Maxim in 1884, which made use of the fired projectile's recoil force to reload. This made it more efficient and less labor-intensive than the Gatling. The first Gatling, which used percussion caps, was supplanted in 1867 by a model using metallic cartridges, which was less prone to jam. This was bought in numbers by the US Army and had a firing rate of 600 rounds per minute.

Gatling, the son of planter and inventor Jordan Gatling, not only invented the gun that bore his name, but also patented a seed-sowing rice planter in 1839 that was later adapted into a successful wheat drill. In 1870, Richard Gatling and his family moved to Hartford, Connecticut, near the Colt Armory where the Gatling gun was manufactured.

By 1876 the Gatling gun had a theoretical rate of fire of 1,200 rounds per minute. Some time later, Gatling-type weapons were invented that diverted a fraction of the gas pressure from the chamber to turn the barrels. Later still, electric motors supplied external power.

New, improved models continued to be produced until the early 20th century when with the advent of the automatic machine gun the US Army declared the Gatling obsolete. The Gatling concept made a comeback, however, in the late 1940s/early 1950s for aircraft; developed versions were also extensively used for air-to-ground operations in the Vietnam War.

AT A GLANCE

Invented during the American Civil War of 1861, the multi-barreled Gatling gun was one of the first machine guns. Weapons using its rotating-barrel concept were still being used a century later in Vietnam, proof of its inventor's forward thinking.

No. 47.631.

R. J. Gatling

Battery Gun.

Patented May. 9. 1865.

1½ Inch to 1 Ft.

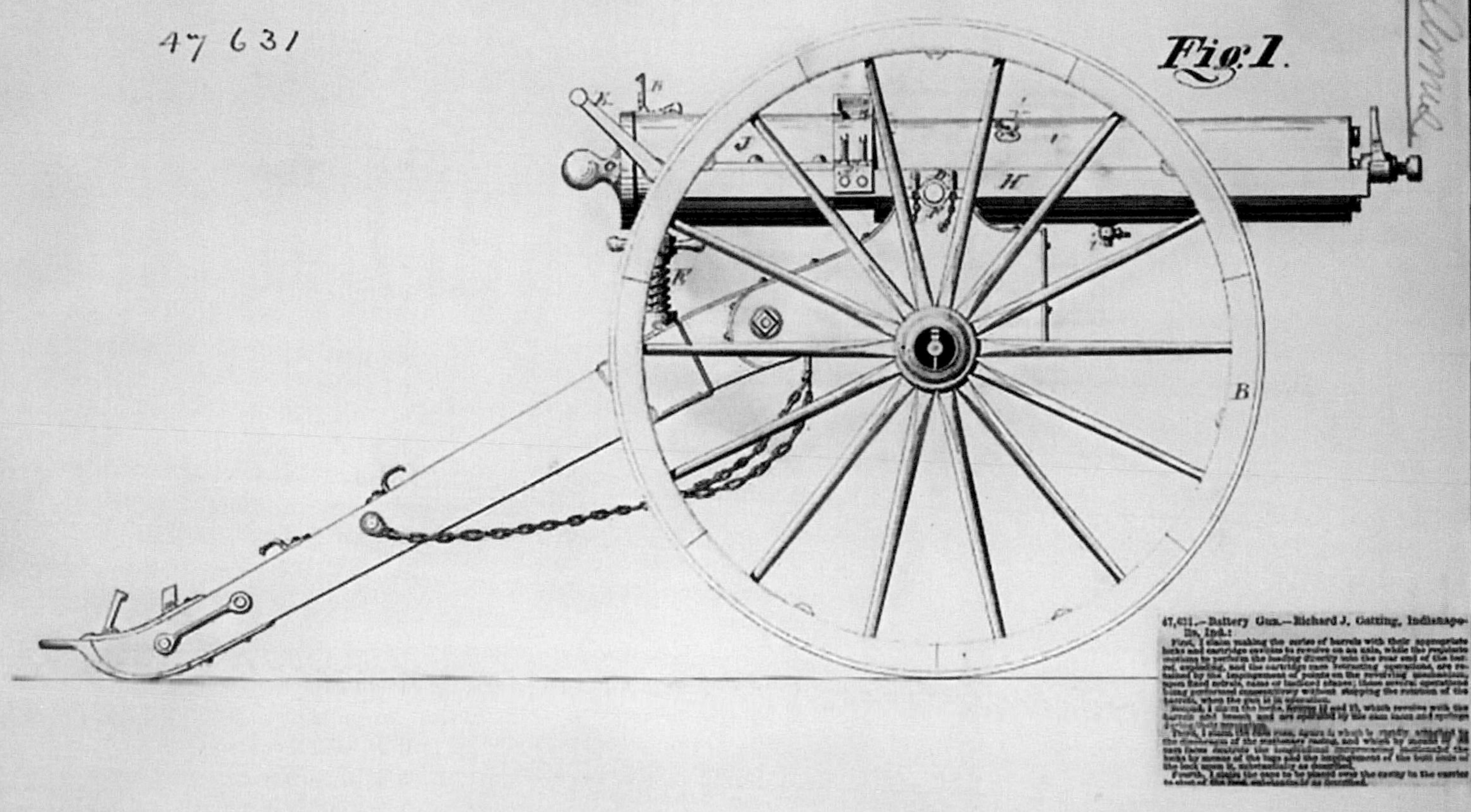

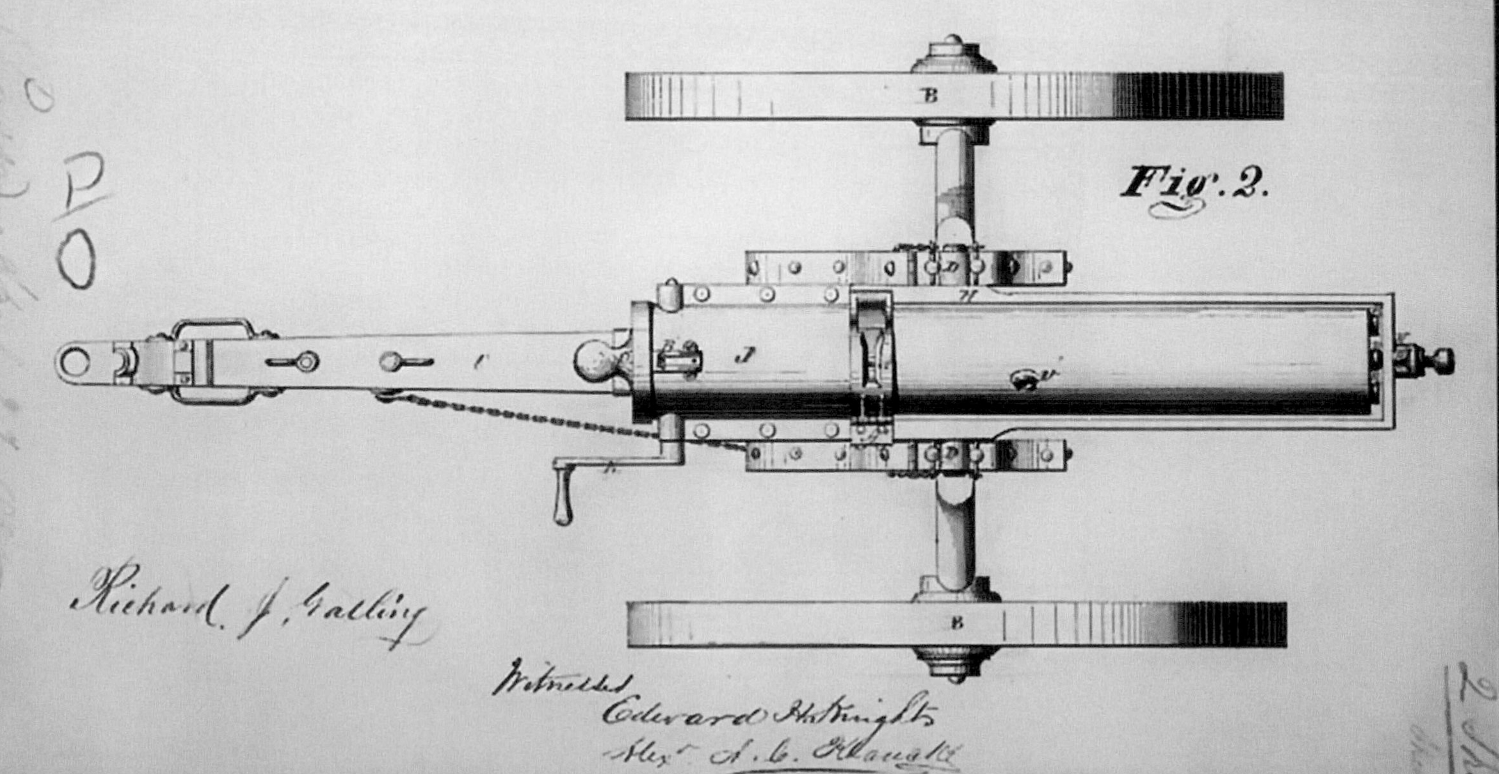

Above: The surrender by Lee to Grant at Appomattox Court House ended the American Civil War.

Right: General Lee poses on his horse, Traveler, after the end of the war.

LEE'S SURRENDER MARKS THE END OF THE AMERICAN CIVIL WAR

APPOMATTOX, VIRGINIA, USA

APRIL 9, 1865

The surrender of Confederate General Robert E. Lee to his Union counterpart, General Ulysses S. Grant, ended the American Civil War to all intents and purposes. They agreed terms during the morning of April 9, 1865, and Lee formally surrendered to Grant shortly after midday. The historic encounter took place at Appomattox Court House, site of the final battle of the Appomattox Campaign, the decisive series of skirmishes which had begun a couple of weeks earlier.

AT A GLANCE

The controversial issue of slavery sparked the American Civil War in 1861, seven Southern (pro-slavery) states having declared their independence from the Union, and another four joining them. Their defeat after a bloody four-year conflict cost over a million military and civilian lives, and the scars on the relatively new nation took a long time to heal.

The origins of the war had lain in the election of Republican Abraham Lincoln, a fervent anti-slavery campaigner, as President of the United States in 1860. Although slavery was being gradually abolished in the North, it remained legal in the Southern states, where it was seen as an important part of the economy. By the time Lincoln took up office in March 1861, seven of those states had already declared their independence from the Union: South Carolina had been the first to secede, in December 1860, followed by Mississippi, Florida, Alabama, Georgia, Louisiana and Texas.

The North responded by calling for a volunteer army from each state of the Union. This led to the border states of Virginia, Arkansas, Tennessee and North Carolina also seceding from the Union, to join the seven Southern states in their newly formed Confederate States of America. Lincoln's government declared that secession was illegal, and refused to recognize the Confederacy as a sovereign state. Hostilities began on April 12, 1861, when Confederate forces captured Fort Sumner, a Union stronghold in Charleston, South Carolina.

The Union quickly seized control of the border states, while Lee made some gains in the east. But in 1863, Union victories at Vicksburg and Gettysburg split the Confederate forces. At that point, the Confederate army had clearly lost the war, but they staggered grimly on for nearly two more years. Their last hope was to reunite Lee's Army of North Virginia with General Joseph E. Johnston's troops in South Carolina, but Lee's defeat at Appomattox in April 1865 prevented this. The remaining Confederate troops surrendered within a month, and the war was declared over by President Andrew Johnson on August 20, 1865.

The civil war was the bloodiest conflict in American history, with 620,000 soldiers killed and an estimated half million civilian lives lost. It was one of the world's first industrialised conflicts, and its use of mass-produced weapons and trench warfare foreshadowed World War I. Victory for the Union meant that in 1865 slavery was abolished throughout the United States by the Thirteenth Amendment to the United States Constitution.

War Department, Washington, April 20, 1865.

$100,000 REWARD!

THE MURDERER

Of our late beloved President, ABRAHAM LINCOLN,

IS STILL AT LARGE.

$50,000 REWARD!

will be paid by this Department for his apprehension, in addition to any reward offered by Municipal Authorities or State Executives.

$25,000 REWARD!

will be paid for the apprehension of JOHN H. SURRATT, one of Booth's accomplices.

$25,000 REWARD!

will be paid for the apprehension of DANIEL C. HARROLD, another of Booth's accomplices.

LIBERAL REWARDS will be paid for any information that shall conduce to the arrest of either of the above-named criminals, or their accomplices.

All persons harboring or secreting the said persons, or either of them, or aiding or assisting their concealment or escape, will be treated as accomplices in the murder of the President and the attempted assassination of the Secretary of State, and shall be subject to trial before a Military Commission and the punishment of DEATH.

Let the stain of innocent blood be removed from the land by the arrest and punishment of the murderers.

All good citizens are exhorted to aid public justice on this occasion. Every man should consider his own conscience charged with this solemn duty, and rest neither night nor day until it be accomplished.

EDWIN M. STANTON, *Secretary of War.*

GEO. F. NESBITT & CO., Printers and Stationers, cor. Pearl and Pine Streets, N. Y.

Above: A poster offers a reward for the apprehension of Lincoln's assassin.

Left: A contemporary illustration of Abraham Lincoln's assassination by John Wilkes Booth.

DEATH OF ABRAHAM LINCOLN

WASHINGTON, DC, USA

APRIL 14, 1865

On Good Friday, April 14, 1865, Abraham Lincoln became the first US President to be assassinated whilst in office. He was shot whilst watching a play in a private box at Ford's Theater, Washington, DC, with his wife and two guests.

Lincoln's assassin was John Wilkes Booth, an actor, Confederate sympathizer and outspoken supporter of slavery. He was outraged by Lincoln's proposal to abolish slavery. With General Lee's defeat at Appomattox, the South had clearly lost the American Civil War, but Booth believed that they could still win it, because, despite the surrender document signed by Lee on April 9, their General Johnston was fighting on. So Booth and his co-conspirators decided to strike a blow for the Confederacy by kidnapping the President and three other high-ranking members of his administration. But then, after he heard Lincoln declare his intention to give former slaves the vote, Booth, enraged, changed his plan to assassination.

Although attempts by others had failed, Booth succeeded. In the theater, he waited for a particular line in the play to raise a loud laugh and muffle the sound of the shot. Lincoln's bodyguard was absent, and Booth was able to creep up close behind the president and shoot him in the back of the head. Lincoln collapsed, to die early the next morning.

After the shooting, Booth jumped down onto the stage shouting, "*Sic semper tyrannis!*" Latin for 'Thus always to tyrants', the state motto of Virginia. Then, despite breaking his ankle, he managed to escape from the theater in the confusion. He fled to Virginia where, on April 26, 1865, he was killed trying to escape from Union soldiers.

Abraham Lincoln was the first Republican president of the USA. Before that he had been a lawyer and a state legislator in Illinois, and he had served as a member of the House of Representatives. He was a vehement opponent of slavery, and his election as president in 1860 sparked the secession of the Southern States and the start of the American Civil War. In 1862, he issued the first Emancipation Proclamation, which freed all slaves in the Confederacy. He was re-elected in a landslide victory in 1864, his main campaign promise being to enact the Thirteenth Amendment, abolishing slavery; this became law in December 1865.

Lincoln's leadership style was strong yet moderate. But his successor Andrew Johnson and the radical Republicans in the Senate imposed tougher terms on the South than Lincoln had planned. So the murder of Lincoln effectively delayed America's healing process, prolonging the bitterness between North and South; reconstruction of the USA as a whole was a long-drawn-out process, taking from 1865 to 1877.

AT A GLANCE

Abraham Lincoln, the first US President to be assassinated in office, was killed in 1865 in an act of revenge for his key role in the American Civil War against the pro-slavery South. He paid the ultimate price for his convictions, but his death could not derail emancipation, nor – as hoped by the assassin – reverse the result of the war.

INVENTION OF DYNAMITE

GERMANY
1866

Alfred Nobel, the Swede whose millions endowed the prizes that bear his name, accumulated much of his wealth by his invention of dynamite. He had enjoyed an eventful childhood, his engineer/inventor father going bankrupt in 1833, the year of Alfred's birth, then taking the family to live in St Petersburg, Russia. In 1850, Nobel's father sent him abroad to study chemical engineering.

Nobel's father's mechanical workshop flourished during the Crimean War but went bust as the war ended. As Alfred, who returned to Sweden in 1863 with his father, searched desperately for new products, Nikolai N Zinin, his chemistry teacher, reminded him of nitroglycerin. This had been invented by Italian chemist Ascanio Sobrero in 1846 but was liquid and thus difficult to handle.

Alfred's younger brother Emil was killed in one of his nitroglycerine experiments in 1864, but Alfred persevered and formed the company Nitroglycerin AB in Stockholm, Sweden. Around this time Nobel also developed a detonator (blasting cap) using a percussive shock rather than heat for ignition.

He set up the Alfred Nobel & Co Factory in Krümmel near Hamburg, Germany, and in 1866 established the United States Blasting Oil Company in the USA. But when the Krümmel plant was destroyed by an explosion, Nobel decided to make nitroglycerin safer for the user.

Experimenting on a raft anchored on the River Elbe, Nobel discovered that by mixing it with *kieselguhr* (a siliceous deposit also known as diatomaceous earth), a paste-like substance was formed that could be inserted into the holes drilled for mining and then ignited.

He called this mixture 'dynamite' and in 1867 received US patent number 78317 for his invention. Dynamite made Nobel's name and was soon used for blasting tunnels, cutting canals and building railways and roads across the globe.

Although he lived in Paris, Nobel travelled widely, and during the 1870s and 1880s built up a network of factories across Europe to manufacture explosives. In 1894, he bought an ironworks at Bofors in Sweden that became the nucleus of the Bofors arms factory.

When he died in 1896 in Italy, Alfred Nobel held 355 patents, in the fields of electrochemistry, optics, biology, and physiology. He left a will dedicating his fortune to create five prizes that would promote peace and honor scientific and cultural achievements; there were to be prizes in the fields of physics, chemistry, medicine, peace and literature. A new prize, the Sveriges Riksbank Prize in Economic Sciences in Memory of Alfred Nobel, was first awarded in 1969.

Above: Alfred Nobel, the Swedish chemist and engineer who invented dynamite and bequeathed his fortune to institute the Nobel Prizes.

Left: Miners insert dynamite into a rock wall to extract iron ore.

AT A GLANCE

Dynamite has been used all over the world to help create railways, roads, tunnels and canals, as well as to demolish and rebuild. Alfred Nobel was the man who invented it, by combining volatile nitroglycerin with silica. It was one of 355 patents he amassed during his eventful lifetime.

Above: A portrait of political thinker and author Karl Marx.

Right: The reading room at the British Museum in London where Marx wrote Das Kapital, *photographed in 1900.*

DAS KAPITAL PUBLISHED

LONDON, UK
1867

Karl Marx is often thought of as the father of modern socialism, and in his most important work, *Das Kapital* (*'Capital'*), he developed his radical theories about class struggle and the economic laws of a capitalist society. Exiled in London, he saw for himself the harsh working conditions and relentless exploitation of the labor force. He was also influenced by the radical political theories of his friend Engels, whose views he largely shared. Researched in the library of the British Museum, the first volume of *Das Kapital* was published in 1867; the rest was uncompleted at his death in 1883.

Marx traced the roots of capitalism back to the time when workers had become separated from the raw materials and land. They were therefore forced to work for owners who had enough money to pay for both materials and land and still make a profit. Products could be highly desirable and costly, but the workers would still only receive the 'exchange value' which was payment related to the labor they put in, not to what the product was worth.

In a capitalist society all the profits go to the owner, whereas the workers' pay is unrelated to the profits and they may have only just enough to live on. Although Marx's sympathies were clearly with the working classes, it was rare for Marx to make moral judgments. It is clear, though, that he believed capitalism was harmful, reducing the workers to wage slaves, many doing a single repetitive task.

The object of the capitalist is to produce a large amount of 'surplus value' – i.e. profit. Much of this profit is then ploughed back into the production of more commodities or services, absorbing more wage earners. In this way capitalism is a self-perpetuating system. Clearly, a return to pre-industrial ways could not happen because the worker was now dependent on the owner for factories and other means of production. Ironically, the workers were actually commodities themselves, selling their labor-power for a daily wage; and there was always going to be a plentiful supply of labor to support capitalism's growth, with a reserve army of the unemployed.

For Marx, modern capitalism was all to do with the pursuit of money as an end in itself. However, he did believe that the system was ultimately unsustainable, leading to a diminishing number of monopoly capitalists who would be overthrown by the working classes (as outlined in the earlier work *The Communist Manifesto*). In fact, he even expected an international socialist revolution in his own lifetime, but he was to be disappointed.

AT A GLANCE

Karl Marx's Das Kapital *is the first detailed examination of capitalism, the way it works and its effects on society. In it, he examines the economic laws that govern its operation, with special emphasis given to the dehumanization of exploited workers. The power of this work is such that its arguments have inspired and inflamed sociologists, economists, historians and revolutionaries to the present day.*

MDCCCLVII

Above: *Canal creator Ferdinand de Lesseps with some of his engineers.*

Right: US navy ships traveling through the Suez Canal.

Below: The official opening of the Suez Canal, depicted by Edouard Riou.

OPENING OF THE SUEZ CANAL

EGYPT

NOVEMBER 17, 1869

The opening of the Suez Canal in November 1869 marked the completion of a ten-year construction project aimed at connecting the Mediterranean Sea to the Red Sea. Ships could now travel between Asia and Europe without having to sail the hazardous thousands of miles around Africa, dramatically improving worldwide trade. The canal, together with the Transcontinental Railway across the United States that had been opened six months earlier, allowed circumnavigation of the globe with previously unknown speed. It also encouraged more European colonization of Africa.

In 1798, Napoleon Bonaparte had discovered evidence of an Ancient Egyptian waterway in the area and considered the construction of a new canal, but he ultimately abandoned the project; it was another Frenchman, Ferdinand de Lesseps, a former diplomat in Egypt, who was to play a major role in developing the canal. In 1854, Egyptian ruler Said Pasha granted de Lesseps a concession to build the waterway. The Suez Canal Company was established for the purpose but, apart from the French, most people in European did not believe the scheme would be feasible, so financial support for it was low.

Work began in April 1859. An estimated 1.5 million people labored on the construction of the canal, with up to 30,000 working at any one time. The use of forced Egyptian labor was a controversial aspect of the project, but even so, when the canal opened to shipping in November 1869, the project had cost more than double its original estimate. Running from Port Said in the north to the city of Suez at its southernmost tip, the canal is 119 miles long. Shipping may move in only one direction at a time, and there are two crossover points: at Ballah By-Pass and the Great Bitter Lake. There are no locks.

Britain purchased Egypt's shares in the Canal Company in 1875. Seven years later, during a civil war in Egypt, British troops moved in to protect British interests in the canal. In 1888, the Convention of Constantinople declared the canal a neutral zone under British protection. In 1936, a treaty with Egypt allowed Britain to continue to retain control, however, Egypt broke this agreement in 1951, and this led to the withdrawal of all British troops in 1956.

That same year, nationalization of the canal by Egypt's President Nasser and the freezing of its assets provoked the Suez Crisis. War was averted by the creation of the first ever United Nations peacekeeping force, to ensure continued international access to the canal. However, during the 1967 Arab–Israeli conflict, the Six Day War, UN troops were withdrawn, and the canal was closed to shipping – with the side-effect of speeding the building of supertankers – until 1975, when it reopened.

AT A GLANCE

Former French diplomat Ferdinand de Lesseps pushed through the development of a canal which, when opened in 1869, meant that ships plying between Asia and Europe no longer had to take the far longer and more hazardous route around Africa. Despite several military conflicts over access through the years, the Suez Canal remains in use today.

DEF
ABC
GHI
JKL
MNO
PRS
TUV
WXY
OPERATOR
SELECT

ALEXANDER GRAHAM BELL DEVELOPS THE TELEPHONE

BOSTON, MASS., USA
MARCH 10, 1876

Edinburgh-born Aleck (Alexander) Bell's father, uncle and grandfather had all worked in the field of elocution, and as a boy Aleck experimented with resonance and the mechanics of speech. At the age of 16, he and his brother built an automaton with adjustable lips and bellows which said the word 'mama'.

Above: Model of Alexander Graham Bell's first electric speaking telephone.

Left: An old-fashioned rotary phone, surrounded by more modern cellphones.

Bell's own interest in the science of sound was spurred on by his mother's deafness, and after the family moved to the USA he taught the Visible Speech System; this had been devised by his father for writing down sounds by showing the actions of tongue, lips and throat, used to help the deaf to speak. In 1873 he was appointed Professor of Vocal Physiology and Elocution at Boston University.

Boston was at the time a melting pot of creative scientific innovation, and Bell was so stimulated by the environment that he took himself to the brink of exhaustion, teaching by day and experimenting through the night. He became obsessed with the idea of transmitting sound by electricity. With no formal training in electronics, he was convinced, after he had misunderstood a German scientific text, that it had already been achieved, and that 'my failure was due only to my ignorance of electricity'. It was not – but without that misreading he might never have pursued the idea.

On February 14, 1876, he filed a patent application for a 'method and apparatus' called the acoustic telegraph, which he had originally devised as a means of sending multiple Morse code telegraph messages down a single wire. He found that the same method could carry the multiple harmonic overtones of speech. On March 10, three days after the patent was granted, he famously used his invention for the first time, to say to his electrical mechanic Thomas Watson, waiting in a neighboring room: 'Mr Watson, come here. I want to see you.'

The Bell Telephone Company was formed in 1877, when Western Union turned down the chance to buy the patent for $100,000 on the basis that the phone was nothing more than a plaything. Within ten years, 150,000 Americans owned a telephone. It made millionaires of Bell and of its investors, and indeed of many others in future years in the massive telecommunications industry which it spawned.

Over the next 18 years Bell Telephone faced over 600 lawsuits from rival claimants to the invention. The company lost none of the cases.

AT A GLANCE

The invention of the telephone by Alexander Graham Bell revolutionized communication as the 19th-century world knew it. Prior to this, Morse code had been the cutting edge of technology. Bell's invention came from techniques for teaching speech to the deaf, and laid the foundations for the mobile communications revolution of a century later.

Above: A photograph shwing the inner workings of a Tesla coil.

Right: Nikola Tesla, the man whose experiments led to use of alternating currents in electrical machinery, in his laboratory, 1910.

NIKOLA TESLA LIGHTS THE CHICAGO WORLD'S FAIR

CHICAGO, USA
1893

Inventor and engineer Nikola Tesla was born in 1856 in the village of Smiljan, then part of the Austro-Hungarian Empire and now in Croatia. Having worked as an electrical engineer in Germany, Hungary and France, he migrated to the USA in 1884 and made many discoveries in the field of electromagnetism in the years that followed.

Tesla worked briefly with fellow inventor Thomas Edison in New Jersey, but they fell out and became bitter rivals. Tesla's system of generating alternating current (AC) electricity had advantages over Edison's direct current system, and this became apparent when George Westinghouse, founder of the Westinghouse Electric Company, bought patent rights to Tesla's system and used it to light the World's Columbian Exposition at Chicago in 1893. Edison's company, General Electric, had also bid for the exposition's lighting contract, but his proposal cost roughly twice as much and would have produced less light and a lot more heat.

The success of Tesla's AC generator was confirmed when Westinghouse gained a contract to build the massive turbines at Niagara Falls. The same principle is still used to provide light and electricity today. The Tesla Coil is used in radios, television sets and a wide range of other electronic equipment; invented in 1891, it has never been improved on. This is the basis for modern AC systems; no electrical system in the world today would work in the same way without Tesla's innovations.

When Tesla became a US citizen in 1891, he was at the peak of his creative powers. His projects included the new types of generators and transformers, a system of AC power transmission, fluorescent light and a new type of steam turbine. He became intrigued by the concept of wireless transmission of power. The Tesla Effect refers to an application of this type of electrical conduction, the movement of energy through space and matter rather than the production of voltage across a conductor.

In 1943, the year of his death, the US Supreme Court upheld Tesla's patent number 645576 in a ruling that served as the basis for patented radio technology in the USA. He had predated Marconi's breakthrough, which he claimed used his patents, but he never saw a penny in compensation. Sadly, despite having sold the rights to his AC system, Tesla died in debt.

AT A GLANCE

Nikola Tesla developed the alternating current system of electricity that is still used today, over a century later. Though derided by many as a 'crazy inventor', his mind can in retrospect be seen as one of the greatest in science. And while his inventions failed to make him rich, his name is celebrated in the Tesla Effect, the term used to describe wireless energy transfer.

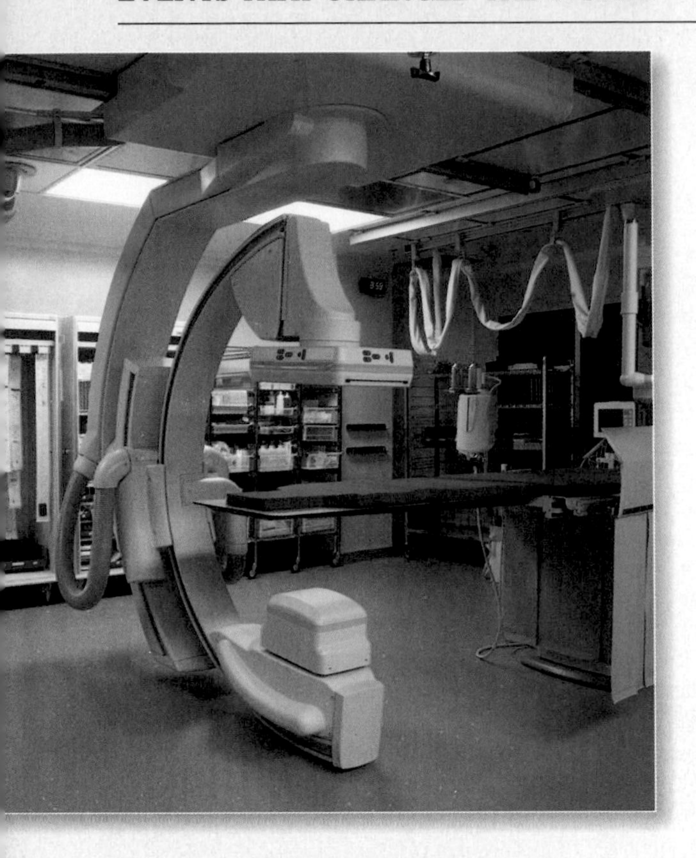

Above: A modern X-ray machine, made possible by the discoveries of Marie Curie.

Right: An illustration of Marie Curie and Pierre Curie in their Paris laboratory.

MARIE CURIE DISCOVERS RADIUM

PARIS, FRANCE
1898

Marie Curie, born in Poland, was a dedicated woman whose work with her husband Pierre would help millions through aiding the development of X-ray technology, and help battle the most feared disease of the late 20th century, cancer.

Marie was born into a highly academic family; her parents were teachers, and it was no surprise when she moved to Paris aged 24 to study at its world-famous university, the Sorbonne. It was here she met and married Pierre Curie and began the research that would change their lives and make their names.

They were continuing the work of physicists Wilhelm Conrad Röntgen and Henri Becquerel; the former had discovered X-rays and the latter radioactivity. Marie and Pierre were researching radioactivity – though the pair had yet to coin the term – in the mineral uraninite.

In exploring the uraninite ore, they removed the radioactive elements uranium and thorium, and while doing so detected a much higher level of radioactivity than before. In June 1898 a new element, hundreds of times more active than uranium, was identified and named polonium, after Marie's native country.

By the end of the year, the Curies had discovered yet another element, this one a million times more radioactive than uranium. They named it radium, and it would be key to their future work. It would later be used as a source of radiation in radiotherapy to prevent cancer cells from dividing, but also had other applications.

After separating it and determining its atomic weight, Curie compiled her research and results into a doctoral thesis. She presented it to her examination committee, two of whose members went on to receive the Nobel Prize in later years; they described it as 'the greatest scientific contribution ever made in a doctoral thesis'.

The Curies were awarded the Nobel Prize for physics in 1903 for their research into radiation begun by Becquerel. After Pierre's sudden death in 1906, Marie carried on her work, becoming the first woman to be made a professor at the Sorbonne and the first person to win two Nobel Prizes, the second being awarded to her in 1911 for her discoveries of polonium and radium.

Curie used her knowledge to aid the war effort in 1914, bringing X-ray machines to the battlefield in vehicles and using radioactive gas to treat diseased tissue. She died in July 1934 from leukemia – a tragic consequence of her many years of close contact with the element she had brought to the world's attention.

Marie's two Nobel Prizes put her in an elite bracket of four multiple winners – a fitting honor for a woman who had dedicated her life to science and left a legacy of hope for sufferers of cancer.

AT A GLANCE

Marie Curie's work opened the doors to many new opportunities in medical research, with X-rays helping to diagnose ailments early, and using radium to help sufferers of many different strains of cancer. Her legacy gave many some people the chance to survive a disease previously untreatable by orthodox medicine.

TAKE-OFF AT KITTY HAWK

NORTH CAROLINA, USA
DECEMBER 17, 1903

A primitive toy helicopter powered by a rubber band, a present from their father in 1878, prompted the young brothers Wilbur and Orville Wright to dream of powered, manned flight. Their mechanical curiosity led them first to design and build a printing press and then to run a bicycle repair shop, from which they manufactured their own bike design. In the 1890s they became fascinated with the pioneers of glider flight, and in 1899 began to carry out their own experiments.

Above: Bicycle mechanics Wilbur and Orville Wright, developers of the world's first practical aircraft.

Left: The famous Wright 1903 Flyer hangs from the ceiling of the National Air and Space Museum in Washington, DC.

Wilbur and Orville knew that the technology to build successful motorized flying machines already existed – more than 20 powered flights had been made in the 19th century. The missing element, they believed, was reliable control by the pilot. So in a series of gliders they concentrated their efforts on devising safe and effective ways of changing direction.

Their great innovation was to steer by banking (tilting the plane sideways when turning, like a bike). Rival flyers kept their plane wings level while steering with a rudder, but the Wrights had observed birds twisting their wings and banking, and used a system of wires to reproduce the effect by warping the wings of their gliders.

All their trials took place on the beach at Kitty Hawk in North Carolina, which had the benefit of constant Atlantic winds for take-off and flight, and soft sands for sudden landings. In 1902, after more than 700 glider flights, they perfected a revolutionary three-axis system for controlling yaw (flat rotation), pitch (tilt up and down forward–backward) and roll (banking).

They then turned to the question of power and devised an early version of a fuel injection engine. They even carved their own propellers, which proved to be up to 82 per cent efficient (modern props have a maximum efficiency of 85 per cent).

On December 17, 1903, there was a cold, strong headwind. Wilbur ran alongside their plane, the Wright Flyer, while Orville piloted that first attempt, reaching a height of 20 feet and proceeding at a stately 6.8 miles per hour, for 12 seconds. This flight, covering 120 feet over the ground, was shorter than the wingspan of a Boeing 747.

The Wright brothers made three more flights that day, finishing and climaxing with Wilbur's 59-second flight over 852 feet of ground. After the last flight, a gust of wind caught the plane and rolled it over several times, wrecking it. The Wright Flyer never flew again, but after that day, humankind could start to dream of the stars.

AT A GLANCE

The 120-foot, 12-second flight Orville Wright made in 1903 ushered in the world of powered flight, because his machine was the first ever to use a practicable control system. Passenger flight, which is now taken for granted, and the supremacy given by air power in wars, both owe their beginnings to his brief hop above the sands at Kitty Hawk in a wood and fabric biplane braced with wires.

EINSTEIN PUBLISHES HIS THEORY OF RELATIVITY

SWITZERLAND
1905

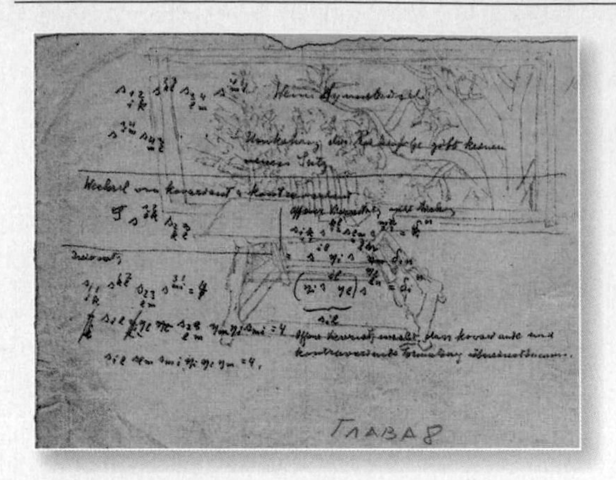

Above: *Hand-written equations and drawing by Albert Einstein.*

Right: Albert Einstein as a young man. He developed the Theory of Special Relativity while still in his twenties.

Below: Einstein and his revolutionary theory.

Albert Einstein was an obscure clerk in the Swiss Patents Office when, in 1905, he published four papers in the prestigious magazine '*Annalen der Physik*' (Annals of Physics). One of these papers, now known as the Special Theory of Relativity, has changed the way we look at our universe.

Born in Germany in 1879, Albert Einstein was the son of a manufacturer of electrical instruments. The family moved to Italy and then to Switzerland. Albert renounced his German citizenship to avoid military service, and studied mathematics and physics at the Polytechnic of Zurich, graduating in 1900. Unable to find a teaching post, he accepted a job at the Patents Office in Bern. He worked as an evaluator of electromagnetic devices, and the knowledge he gained led him to come up with his theories of relativity. In 1905, he received his doctorate from the University of Zurich.

That same year, his Theory of Special Relativity brought him to the attention of the world. This and subsequent ground-breaking work such as his theory of General Relativity saw him hailed as the father of modern physics; he became one of the most famous and recognizable scientists in the world. Einstein's genius was not limited to physics; he also published papers on politics and philosophy. He is quoted as saying: 'the true sign of intelligence is not knowledge but imagination'.

The Special Theory is based on the premise that motion is relative, and also that matter cannot exceed the speed of light; the nearer matter approaches that speed, the more massive it becomes. This is expressed in the famous equation $E = mc^2$, E being energy (measured in joules), m mass (measured in kilograms), and c the speed of light (measured in meters per second). Einstein also proposed that the closer an object gets to the speed of light the more time, *as far as that object is concerned*, slows down.

Although Einstein had been influenced by other scientists like Isaac Newton, Henri Poincaré and James Clerk Maxwell, his work was a radical departure from tradition. Physicist Max Planck was the first to recognize the significance of Special Relativity, and his support led to its wider acceptance.

Einstein incorporated gravity into the theory, to arrive at General Relativity in 1915. This went beyond Newton's laws of gravity and introduced a universe of warped space and time, from which have sprung the ideas of black holes, wormholes and white holes. His work on the photoelectric effect won him a Nobel Prize in 1921.

Fleeing Germany in 1933 to escape the Nazis, Einstein became an American citizen in 1940, and he resided in New Jersey till his death in April 1955.

AT A GLANCE

Albert Einstein's Special Theory of Relativity was published in 1905, and it changed the way we look at our universe. Based on the premise that motion is relative and that matter cannot exceed the speed of light, it is expressed by the famous equation $E = mc^2$.

Above: French pioneer Louis Blériot, the first person to fly across the English Channel.

Right: Blériot , accompanied by his wife, surveys where his monoplane came to rest on a Dover hillside, winning him a £1,000 prize.

Below: Louis Bleriot (left), with fellow flight pioneer Charles Lindbergh in 1927.

LOUIS BLÉRIOT FLIES THE CHANNEL

CALAIS, FRANCE–DOVER, ENGLAND

JULY 25, 1909

When French aviator Louis Blériot flew across the English Channel on July 25, 1909, he became the first person to complete a flight across a large body of water in a heavier-than-air machine. This crucial moment in the story of aviation came less than six years after the Wright brothers had achieved their record for manned, powered heavier-than-air flight – lasting for nearly a minute, covering over 850 ft along the ground – in December 1903 at Kitty Hawk.

The British *Daily Mail* offered a £1,000 reward for the first successful cross-channel flight, the latest in a series of prizes offered by the newspaper for aviation feats. Blériot had two rivals: the favorite, Hubert Latham, was a Frenchman, while Count Charles de Lambert was a Russian aristocrat and a protégé of Wilbur Wright. Latham was the first to attempt the crossing, but in his flight on July 19 his plane developed engine trouble and he ended by ditching in the sea six miles short of Dover. Meanwhile, de Lambert had injured himself during a test flight, so was out of the contest.

An engineer and inventor, Blériot had been building aircraft since 1903. He had created the world's first monoplane, but this, like most of his early prototypes, was unstable in flight. His most successful monoplane models were the Blériot VII and XI, but a problem with the VII left Blériot with a badly burned foot and also meant that only the XI was available. The channel crossing was to be its maiden flight.

On July 25, as Latham slept, Blériot took to the air at 4.30 a.m. Although he had been told the weather conditions were safe, he quickly found himself in difficulties. He was being escorted by a French navy destroyer, but soon lost sight of the ship. Flying in thick fog without the aid of a compass, Blériot had no alternative but to fly blind, steering as straight and level as he could. The 21-mile trip from Calais to Dover took around 37 minutes, and a rain shower cooled the engine so much that it was in danger of stalling. Sighting the English coast and a French reporter waving the tricolor flag of France to show him where to touch down, Blériot performed an awkward landing. Although this damaged his plane's undercarriage, Blériot was uninjured and the landing was judged a success. So Blériot was awarded the prize, and instant celebrity followed.

He continued to design and build aircraft throughout World War I. Louis Blériot died in August 1936.

AT A GLANCE

Frenchman Louis Blériot's success in flying the English Channel in just over half an hour in a 'stick-and-string' monoplane made Britain realise it could no longer rely on the seas to protect it. Astonishingly, it was the aircraft's maiden flight and came only six years after the Wright brothers' brief hop at Kitty Hawk.

SINKING OF THE *TITANIC*

NORTH ATLANTIC
APRIL 14, 1912

It's hard to imagine the shock and terror of the passengers of the RMS *Titanic* on that freezing April night when at long last they realized that the ship, having struck an apparently inconsequential iceberg, was doomed to sink. There had been a party atmosphere about the journey – the maiden voyage of the biggest, most luxurious ship in the world at the time. Confident celebration had been the order of the day. But such confidence was misplaced.

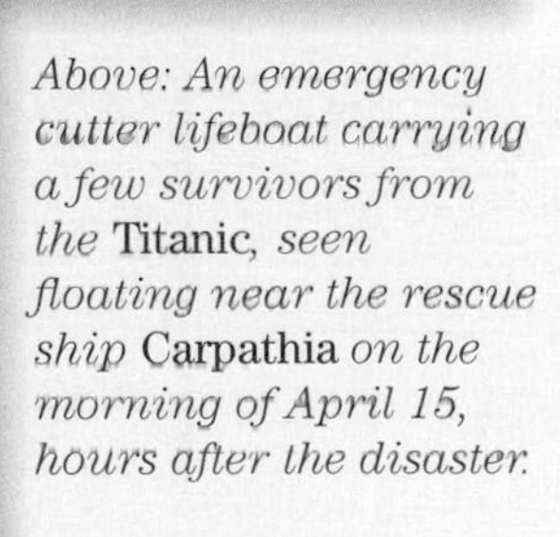

Above: An emergency cutter lifeboat carrying a few survivors from the Titanic, *seen floating near the rescue ship* Carpathia *on the morning of April 15, hours after the disaster.*

Left: The Titanic *sails away from the dock prior to her ill-fated maiden voyage.*

Although the *Titanic* was 882 ft 9 inches (269.1 metres) long by 92 foot (28 metres) wide, it was in fact, far from invulnerable. For example, the rudder was too small to steer such a large ship while it was steaming at full speed, and this was normal practice in the ice fields, where it was felt that any iceberg big enough to sink a ship would be spotted in ample time to take evasive action. Furthermore, only two of the three propellers could be put into reverse, also inadequate for such a massive ship. Ironically, in the event, the order to reverse given by Captain Edward Smith, the ship's master, reduced the rudder's effect even more.

The *Titanic,* as trade journals reported in advance of its departure, was 'practically unsinkable' thanks to its electrically controlled system of watertight bulkheads dividing it into 16 compartments below the waterline. The ship was designed to withstand up to any two compartments, or the first four, being flooded; it was appallingly bad luck that because the ship had slewed to avoid the iceberg, its side hit the berg with such force that it struck the plates of the hull across five compartments. Even then, the damage might have been limited had the rivets securing the plates not been substandard; it was the rivets, not the iron sheets, that gave way, opening up gaping holes for the icy North Atlantic to pour into.

Of the 2,223 passengers and crew on board, only 706 survived. Even if all the lifeboats launched had been filled to capacity, there were nothing like enough of them, and most victims died from hypothermia after around 15 minutes of immersion in the dark, numbing waters. Among so many sad stories, one of the saddest was that of Nils Pållson, a Swede waiting on the quayside in New York for the arrival of his wife Alma and their four young children, who were travelling in third class; he lost his whole family.

The *Titanic* had complied fully with all the safety regulations of the day, which subsequent government enquiries decided were thoroughly out of date. The enduring legacy of the sinking was the complete revision of those standards. The enormity of the disaster and the loss of life in the face of the optimism generated by the maiden voyage of this iconic vessel have ensured our continuing fascination with the tragedy a century later.

AT A GLANCE

The loss of the 'practically unsinkable' Titanic *in 1912 has passed into folklore and has inspired books, films and museum exhibits to commemorate it. The only silver lining from the loss of over 1,500 people was the revision of safety standards that had until then allowed ships to run the gauntlet of iceberg fields and other navigational hazards in the belief that they could survive almost any collision.*

Above: The assassination of Franz Ferdinand in Sarajevo as depicted by I.B. Hazelton.

Right: An illustration of soldiers arresting Gavrilo Princip, assassin of the Archduke Franz Ferdinand in Sarajevo.

ASSASSINATION OF ARCHDUKE FRANZ FERDINAND

SARAJEVO, SERBIA
JUNE 28, 1914

June 28 had long been a significant date in the Serbian national calendar, being the anniversary of the Battle of Kosovo in 1389 which had resulted in Serbia's loss of independence. Early in the 20th century, Serbian separatists of the Black Hand Organization planned to use the date to strike a blow for their cause, and a visit in 1914 by Archduke Franz Ferdinand to inspect troops in Sarajevo presented them with a golden opportunity. After the suicide of his cousin Rudolf in 1889, Franz Ferdinand had become heir to the imperial crown of the Austro-Hungarian Empire.

His assassination had been meticulously planned. Six men were stationed along the route of the Archduke's morning motorcade through Sarajevo. Although the first two lost their nerve, the third threw a grenade – but it failed to kill Franz Ferdinand because he batted it away with his arm. It exploded in front of the following car, and the thrower of the bomb was quickly captured. The sound of the explosion, however, convinced the remaining three conspirators that their efforts would no longer be required.

After lunch, the distressed Archduke decided that he and his wife would visit in hospital those injured by the grenade. By chance, his car passed a café just as Gavrilo Princip, one of the three remaining assassins, emerged from it and recognized him. Still armed with a pistol, Princip ran towards the vehicle and fired twice: the first bullet struck Franz Ferdinand in the neck, and the second hit his wife Sophie in the abdomen. As they both collapsed, the Archduke begged his duchess, 'Don't die! Don't die! Stay alive, for our children!' The car raced to the governor's residence, but the couple died within 15 minutes of each other.

Austria-Hungary, outraged, declared war on Serbia. Then Germany and Italy – the two other members of its military partnership known as the Triple Alliance – backed Austria-Hungary. Imperial Russia declared its support for Serbia, and was joined by Britain and France, Russia's allies in their partnership, the Triple Entente. Italy eventually chose to join the Entente forces.

The Great War which followed transformed the map of Europe. Russian losses during the war fueled the Russian Revolution and the rise of the Soviet Union. At the end of the war, the Austro-Hungarian Empire was dismantled, the Balkan borders were redrawn and the punitive Treaty of Versailles led directly to the rise of Hitler, and so to the Second World War and the Cold War. All these changes were triggered by an opportunistic bullet hitting an accidental heir.

AT A GLANCE

The opportunist assassination of Archduke Franz Ferdinand of Austria in June 1914 lit the touch paper on the First World War. When Austria declared war on Serbia, their respective allies, the stage was set for the map of Europe to be redrawn.

SINKING OF THE *LUSITANIA*

IRELAND

MAY, 1915

The *Lusitania*, a British passenger liner, was sailing from New York to Liverpool in May 1915 when it was sunk by a German U-boat submarine. Prior to this event, the German government had published an article in New York newspapers warning that all vessels flying the flag of Britain or her allies were in danger of destruction if they entered the war zone. But not everybody heeded this advice. This fast modern liner, owned by Cunard, was hit by a torpedo, and it sank. Including passengers and crew, 1,198 people died, accounting for more than half of those on board. Significantly, 128 American citizens died, victims of a war in which they were not involved. This event caused great ill-feeling towards Germany and was instrumental in America entering the war two years later.

As the liner approached the coast of Ireland, coming to the end of its journey, the U-boat struck. A torpedo hit the side of the liner and the 'greyhound of the seas' was doomed. There was mass panic on board. The lifeboats proved cumbersome, some even falling on top of the passengers on deck. Lowering the lifeboats into the sea proved almost impossible due to the speed the liner was travelling at, and many overloaded lifeboats tipped their occupants into the sea.

In America, condemnation was swift and unforgiving. It was argued that attacking a non-military vessel broke international agreements. The Germans countered this argument by saying that it was common knowledge that the liner was carrying explosives to help the British war effort. The US authorities denied this. The truth can only be guessed at. Many survivors told of hearing two great explosions, whereas the U-boat's Captain Schwieger logged only one torpedo as having been fired. Some maintain that the second explosion was caused by an illegal cargo of high explosives.

In Britain there were hopes that the USA would now enter the war, but its president, Woodrow Wilson, was more restrained in his views. He did insist, though, that Germany must apologize and cease its attacks on commercial vessels whatever flag they were flying. The Germans agreed. However, in August 1915 a German submarine torpedoed the British liner SS *Arabic* with the loss of 44 lives, including three US citizens. This confirmed that the sinking of the *Lusitania* had not been an isolated incident, and the USA's entry into the war was now inevitable.

Above: Created by Bernard Partridge, this poster typifies the British and the US (to a lesser extent) outrage felt at the sinking of a civilian vessel.

Right:: The liner Lusitania *pictured in New York prior to her transatlantic crossing.*

In 1915 the sinking of the British Lusitania *shocked the world. En route from New York to Liverpool it was torpedoed and sunk by a German submarine. Many people died, including over 100 US citizens. Although explicit warnings had been given, the brutality of this attack was unexpected; it hardened feeling against Germany, eventually leading to US involvement in World War I.*

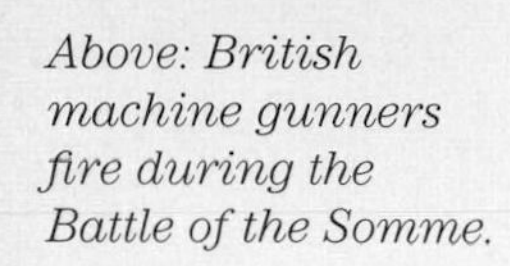

Above: British machine gunners fire during the Battle of the Somme.

Left: British troops would go 'over the top' to almost certain death.

FIRST DAY OF THE BATTLE OF THE SOMME

NORTHERN FRANCE
JULY 1, 1916

The Somme Offensive of 1916 was conceived as a counter-attack intended to breach the lines of the German Army, which had occupied northern France since 1914.

Defenders of the campaign argue that it was essential to prepare the ground for the subsequent defeat of Germany, and that it was a useful learning exercise in tactical and operational issues – in effect, a handy lesson in how not to do it. The campaign, however, failed in its objectives, and on the first day alone 20 per cent of Britain's entire fighting force was killed, the worst loss ever sustained by the British army.

On that single day, an estimated 19,240 British servicemen died. Britain's total losses for the day, including those wounded, missing or captured, ran to about 57,470. To that horrifying total should be added the 7,000 losses of the smaller French force involved, and another 10,200 of the German front line.

Germany had been expecting a major counter-offensive. Its army had been virtually unchallenged since the invasion, and now commanded high ground on which it was securely dug in. The German trenches were deep and wide, and created effective cover against the week-long barrage which preceded the infantry attack. The British bombardment had been made even less effective by their lack of heavy artillery, the inaccuracy of the British gunners and the wrong shells having been provided: even if the shells had landed on target, only 900 tons of the 12,000 fired were capable of damaging the enemy defenses.

Worse yet, the Garman barbed wire had not been destroyed – broken and tangled, it was an even more lethal trap than before. British troops had been told that thanks to the bombardment all they would have to do would be to walk over to the German lines. But in fact the Germans were still in a commanding position, and most of the soldiers who died were trapped by the wire and killed quickly – if they were lucky – by machine guns.

Poor communication also took its toll. One British officer mistook a German flare for a British signal indicating success, and deployed his reserves, the 801 men of the 1st Newfoundland Regiment. Just a few men of that volunteer force returned unscathed; nearly 300 were wounded, and 500 died – almost an entire generation of men from that Canadian province.

After ten days of fighting, the French had advanced about six miles into German-held territory, whereas the British had made no significant advance. Five months later, by the end of November, despite repeated assaults, this position had hardly changed, and the losses on both sides at the end of the Battle of the Somme had amounted to about 1.2 million men.

AT A GLANCE

The futility of trench warfare was underlined by the British Somme Offensive of 1916 which, thanks to a catalog of errors and a lack of the information needed to make decisions, saw nearly 20,000 men lose their life in a single day, with no ground gained to show for their sacrifice. It was the worst loss ever sustained by the British army, and remains a sobering statistic today.

Above: A crowd of workers and soldiers gather in front of the Winter Palace to hear Lenin speak.

Left: Soldiers prepare in Palace Square as the Russian Revolution gathers momentum.

ATTACK ON THE WINTER PALACE

PETROGRAD, RUSSIA
OCTOBER 25, 1917

Military setbacks in the First World War and economic hardship at home were fueling resentment and dissatisfaction among the Russian people. In February 1917, after a wave of strikes that had been violently suppressed, Tsar Nicholas II was forced to abdicate. A new provisional government was formed by members of the Duma, the Russian Parliament, with its seat in the former tsar's Winter Palace in Petrograd (which had been called St Petersburg until the First World War, and is now once again known by that name). The working classes favored a system of workers' councils, called Soviets. There followed a tense Period of Dual Power, during which the provisional government ruled while reluctantly acknowledging the influence and power of the Soviets.

In April 1917, however, Vladimir Ilyich Ulyanov – Lenin – returned to Petrograd from exile in Switzerland; his arrival galvanized support for the radical Bolshevik factions within the Soviets. After a power struggle within the Soviets, the Bolsheviks won, forming the Soviet workers' militia, the Red Guards (the future Red Army).

The government's determination to continue the war with Germany, and its failure to address the country's economic crisis, led to a new wave of strikes across the country. In August the Red Guards thwarted a military coup, and the Bolsheviks' status as defenders of the people was confirmed. They were seen as the only organized opposition which had not compromised in their dealings with the government – and Lenin knew their time had come.

The first revolutionary action was a Bolshevik uprising in Tallinn (now in Estonia) on October 23, 1917. Two days later, Red Guards took over government offices in Petrograd with little opposition, while government ministers retreated to the Winter Palace. They cobbled together an inadequate defense force of Cossacks and soldiers from the Women's Battalion and waited for the inevitable. A blank shell fired from the battleship Aurora signaled the final assault on the Palace, and it fell in the small hours of the following morning.

The power struggle which followed the overthrow of the provisional government led to five years of civil war across Russia. Only in 1922 was the Soviet Union finally created. But the storming of the Winter Palace in 1917 had been, like the storming of the Bastille at the start of the French Revolution, a symbolic overthrow of the old order. When the Bolsheviks' control over Russia was consolidated, and the traditional European powers decayed after two world wars, the stage was set for the Soviet Union to emerge as a 20th-century superpower.

AT A GLANCE

In the same way as the storming of the Bastille in 1789 had represented the French claim to freedom, so the storming of the Winter Palace in 1917 symbolised the end of the Russian monarchy and the establishment of a new order, which became the Union of Soviet Socialist Republics. This would endure more or less unchanged until the last decade of the 20th century.

FIRST TANK BATTLE

CAMBRAI, FRANCE
NOVEMBER 20, 1917

The Romans had started it, with their *testudo*, then in the 1500s Leonardo da Vinci had sketched a proposal for an armored war machine; and since the 1830s the idea had been bandied about – in 1855, an engineer had drawn plans for one for use in the Crimean War. But the terrain created by trench warfare in the First World War made the rapid development of tanks an urgent priority. Early British prototypes were tested during the later phases of the Somme Offensive. Rushed into service, they were liable to break down; only nine of the 49 Mark I tanks deployed at the Somme in 1916 reached the German lines. More seriously, perhaps, their use in that battle gave away to the enemy the secret of their existence.

Above: A British tank advances towards enemy trenches in France.

Right: British tanks move slowly but surely towards the front line.

Below: A British tank rolls over a trench during the Battle of Cambrai in 1917.

But the trials did provide useful information for subsequent improvements to their reliability and effectiveness. A little over a year later, at Cambrai, large numbers of tanks were incorporated into a battle plan for the first time: they were to be used in a full-scale assault on the strongly defended German positions of the Hindenburg Line in northern France.

381 Mark IV tanks from 12 battalions were involved, and immediately proved their worth, breaching the German defenses and advancing up to five miles into enemy-held territory – a greater advance in six hours than the Allies had achieved in the three months before. Furthermore the casualty rate – 4,000 on that first day – was half that of the recent action at Passchendaele.

Mechanical difficulties persisted, and at the end of the first day 180 tanks were out of action, only 65 of them destroyed by German fire. More tanks were lost when a canal bridge which their unit had successfully taken collapsed under their weight, making further progress on that front impossible.

Germany was quick to reinforce, resisting further British advances and eventually driving them back almost exactly to their lines before the battle. After two weeks of grueling stalemate, both sides had lost around 45,000 men and gained almost no ground.

However, at Cambrai the point had been made that even well defended trenches could be overcome in an attack by tanks, with far fewer casualties than by infantry alone. Public opinion would never again accept human losses on the scale of the War to End All Wars. The art of war was changing; since then, wars have increasingly been fought with modern technology on both sides rather than with the unprotected bodies of men ordered to face mechanised defence systems.

AT A GLANCE

The introduction of the tank to battlefield warfare in the later stages of the First World War revolutionized the way future conflicts would be conducted. The tank's combination of defensive armor, offensive firepower and mobility added a new dimension to ground warfare that would be exploited even further in wars to come.

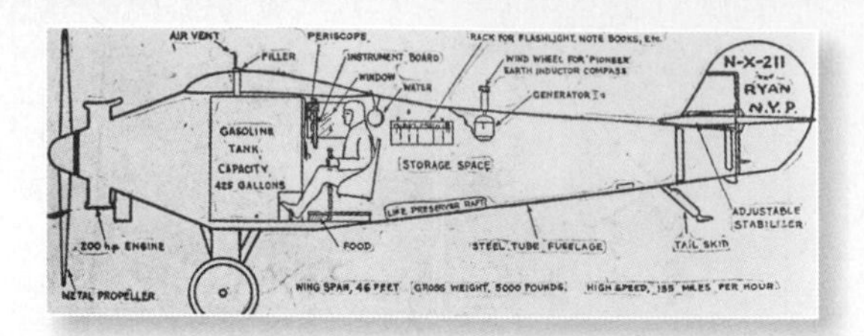

Above: A diagram showing the interior layout of Charles Lindbergh's Spirit of St. Louis *airplane.*

Right: Charles Lindbergh standing beside the Spirit of St. Louis.

Below: An American stamp commemorates Lindbergh's trailblazing flight.

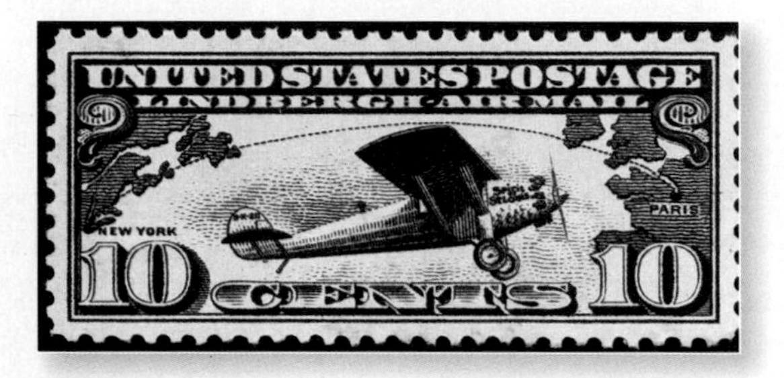

LINDBERGH FLIES THE ATLANTIC SOLO

PARIS, FRANCE

MAY 21, 1927

In 1919, Raymond Orteig, French owner of the Lafayette Hotel in New York, offered a prize of US $25,000 to the first pilot to fly between Paris and New York, in either direction. Aviation was entering a golden age of aeronautical advances, spurred on by public fascination with the new form of transport and by prizes such as that dangled by Orteig.

In 1909, only six years after the Wright Brothers' record-breaking flight, Louis Blériot had won the £1,000 offered by the British *Daily Mail* for the first flight across the English Channel. Just a month after Orteig's prize was announced, two British aviators, Alcock and Brown, flying from Newfoundland in Canada to Ireland, had collected the same newspaper's £10,000 reward for the first flight across the Atlantic. Their success, in just under 16 hours, had only been possible because Brown had climbed out onto the wings to chip ice off the engines while Alcock piloted the plane.

Despite the need for a two-man team, Charles Lindbergh was determined to win the Orteig Prize with a solo effort. By the time, eight years later, he took off from Roosevelt Field outside New York on May 20, 1927, six other airmen had died in their attempts at the prize. But Lindbergh was a courageous and skilled flyer, an airmail pilot and former stunt-flying barnstormer. Overcoming fog, ice, exhaustion, disorientation, storms at altitude and waves at sea level, he landed nearly 34 hours later at Paris's Le Bourget airfield, hailed by a crowd of 200,000. His cramped monoplane, *Spirit of St. Louis,* was half the length of Alcock and Brown's converted First World War heavy bomber, with only two-thirds of the wingspan, and his flight had lasted twice as long as theirs.

Above all, he was the first man to fly solo across the Atlantic – a feat which captured the public imagination, gave him instant fame, and helped transform flying from a military activity and a thrill-seeker's entertainment into a form of mass transport. On his return to New York, Lindbergh's tickertape parade was watched by four million people. In the course of the year-long tour of the United States which followed, it is estimated that 30 million people – a quarter of the population – turned out to see him.

Lindbergh became a passionate advocate of aviation for commerce and travel. In the six months after his achievement, pilot license applications in the USA rose threefold, and the number of licensed aeroplanes in the country increased by a factor of four. By 1929, there were 30 times more air passengers than in 1926, before Lindbergh's flight. Charles Lindbergh's spirited adventure had ushered in the Air Age.

AT A GLANCE

Charles Lindbergh's achievement in flying across the Atlantic solo in 1927 demonstrated the potential of air transport to shrink the globe. It also inspired many Americans to take to the air as private pilots.

Spirit
of
t.Louis

AL JOLSON
2 30 TWICE DAILY 8 4
Sunday Matinees 3 P.
WARNER
WARNERS' THEATRE
WARNERS
AL JOLSON
"THE JAZZ SINGER"
NOW PLAYING
SUPREME TRIUMPH
"THE JAZZ SINGER"

Above: Al Jolson in The Jazz Singer, *the first feature film 'talkie'.*

Left: A huge crowd waits outside Warners' Theater in New York to see The Jazz Singer.

FIRST TALKING PICTURE

NEW YORK, USA
OCTOBER 6, 1927

Warner Bros chose to premiere *The Jazz Singer* on October 6, 1927, the eve of *Yom Kippur*, the Jewish holiday at the center of the movie's plot. In it, the son of a Jewish cantor is torn between his religious duties, the hopes of his parents and the secular stage; in the end he cancels a jazz performance to sing the *Kol Nidre* in the synagogue.

It was not the first sound film; two Warner releases in 1926 had included music and sound effects. Nor was it the first talkie; Fox had released short drama and news reels in May 1927 using the Movietone sound format. But it was the world's first full-length feature film with audible dialogue – a full two minutes of it in a running time of nearly an hour and a half.

Most of the dialogue in the film still needed to be read by the audience on captions as usual. But the film contained 11 songs. Warner Bros favored the Vitaphone recording system, which meant that every song and dialogue sequence was on a different reel, each accompanied by a soundtrack on disc. The projectionist – surely the unsung star of the movie – had to thread 15 reels and cue up 15 discs with split-second accuracy in the course of each 89-minute showing.

The first words spoken by the film's star, Al Jolson, 17 minutes into the movie, were his catch phrase, "You ain't heard nothin' yet." Loud excitement from the audience greeted this and each new section of dialogue. At the end of the film the crowd spilled onto the street chanting "Jolson! Jolson! Jolson!" It was clear to everyone that a new film era had begun.

The Jazz Singer was a phenomenal success. Although it had cost Warner over $400,000 to produce, it grossed over $2,500,000, almost $1,000,000 more than the studio's previous highest earner. Warner received a special Academy Award for the pioneering film, and it was clear that the public wanted more, so Warner moved fast and in July 1928 released the first all-talking feature film, *Lights of New York*.

The rush by every studio to convert to sound production is affectionately and accurately portrayed in the 1952 film *Singin' in the Rain*. Within two years of the *Jazz Singer* premiere, silent films were no longer being produced. Silent film stars whose voices did not record well found themselves out of work. And the stage version of *The Jazz Singer*, on tour at the time of the film premiere, closed when its $3 seats could not compete with the 50c ticket queues at the movie theaters.

AT A GLANCE

The year of the silent movie gave way to the talkies in 1927 when Al Jolson's The Jazz Singer *hit the screens. Its hour and a half required extreme dexterity from the projectionist to line up the sound track discs, but within a decade Hollywood as we know it was up and running.*

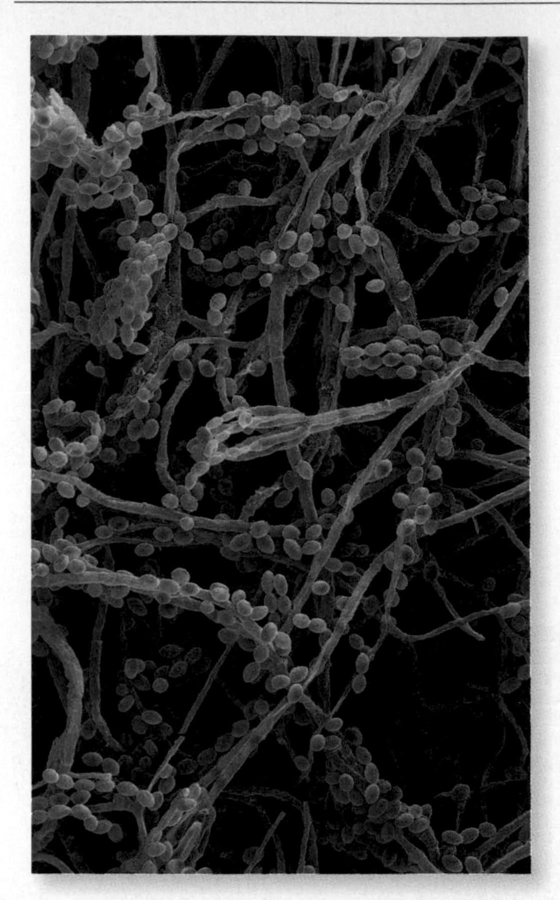

Above: A microscopic view of penicillium *mould spores, from which the antibiotic penicillin is derived.*

Right: Dr Alexander Fleming, the man who discovered penicillin, pictured in his lab in Paddington, London.

ALEXANDER FLEMING DISCOVERS PENICILLIN

PADDINGTON, LONDON, UK

1928

It took a series of chance events to facilitate the discovery that would kick-start 20th-century medicine. When Scottish biologist Alexander Fleming took a two-week break in 1928, he left his work unattended at St Mary's Hospital Medical School in Paddington, London. Upon his return, the contents of his discarded culture plate displayed a culture at work that would go on to be known as penicillin.

Fleming had been pursuing his own theory that nasal mucus could fight bacteria. He had been growing micro-organisms and attacking it with the bodily fluid, which contained the antibacterial enzyme lysozyme.

On returning from his holiday, he discovered that a plate of staphylococcus bacteria that he had left untreated had mould growing on it – and a clear ring surrounded the bacteria showed that they had been destroyed. The plate having been left in the open air had allowed the mould to flourish, releasing a property called *penicillium notatum*, which was fighting the staphylococcus on the plate. While Fleming had been on holiday, a significant scientific event was taking place in his absence.

Instantly realizing the importance of his discovery, Fleming quickly went about determining what this antibacterial agent was. He named the active element penicillin; it was a landmark moment in medicine, as bacterial diseases such as tuberculosis and typhoid fever were at the time going untreated and generating high fatality rates. The potency of this new substance could save millions of lives.

Though credited with the discovery of penicillin, Fleming found it hard to cultivate and, with little initial interest from the scientific community, he decided in 1940 to halt his efforts to develop it as a drug. It was shortly before this, in 1939, that Australian pharmacologist Howard Florey led a team that continued Fleming's work and ultimately led to its mass production.

Florey and his team were able to purify penicillin in amounts that allowed them to carry out experiments on mice and, later, humans that proved its antibacterial effects. The world of science finally took notice, and penicillin was mass produced in the USA. By the time the Second World War ended in 1945, penicillin had been used to treat millions of injured soldiers.

Florey, Fleming and biochemistry expert Ernst Boris Chain were awarded the Nobel Prize for medicine in 1945 for their roles in the discovery and application of penicillin. And millions of lives might not have been saved if Fleming had been a little tidier.

AT A GLANCE

A chance occurrence in Alexander Fleming's laboratory in 1928 led to his discovery of one of medicine's most widely used and useful antibacterial agent. Penicillin is now taken for granted, but has saved millions of lives in eight decades.

STAGE BROADWAY SCREEN

VARIETY

PRICE 25¢

VOL. XCVII. No. 3 NEW YORK, WEDNESDAY, OCTOBER 30, 1929 88 PAGES

WALL ST. LAYS AN EGG

Going Dumb Is Deadly to Hostess In Her Serious Dance Hall Profesh

DROP IN STOCKS ROPES SHOWMEN

Kidding Kissers in Talkers Burns Up Fans of Screen's Best Lovers

Hunk on Winchell

Many Weep and Call Off Christmas Orders — Legit Shows Hit

MERGERS HALTED

Talker Crashes Olympus

Above: A headline announcing the stock market crash of October 29, 1929.

Right: Panicked stock traders crowd the sidewalks outside the New York Stock exchange on the day of the market crash.

WALL STREET CRASH

NEW YORK, USA
OCTOBER 29, 1929

After the horrors of the First World War, a giddy optimism overtook most of the world. The Roaring Twenties was a time of hedonistic excess and prosperity which made people feel financially invincible, almost immortal. From 1923, share prices rose steadily for six years.

Profit on the stock market seemed to be a sure thing, and if you didn't have the money to invest in speculation there was always a stockbroker to lend you some 'on a margin'. At the height of the boom, brokers were prepared to lend two-thirds of the value of shares to new investors – and by 1929 the level of loans (more than $8.5 billion) exceeded the amount of US currency in circulation. It was an overstretched bubble ready to burst.

On September 3, 1929, the Dow Jones Index, peaking at 381.17, began a long, stumbling, painful decline. It finally bottomed out nearly three years later, on July 8, 1932, at 41.22, 89 per cent lower than at its peak. Shares would not return to their 1929 levels until 1954. What had started as a slight reverse on September 4, 1929, continued for a month before the market staged a faltering recovery in mid-October. But confidence had been fatally shaken by the fall, and in late October panic set in. As prices crashed, investors sought to sell their shares as quickly as possible to minimize their losses.

One terrible day has become immortalized as Black Tuesday. In that single day, October 29, 1929, the Dow Jones fell by 12 per cent, and a incredible 16 million shares were traded at the stock exchange – a record unbeaten until 1968. But Black Tuesday set another record; the value of the stock market fell by $14 billion.

One in six American households (belonging to the 16 per cent of the population who played the market) were directly affected by the crash. But worse was to come. Debate still rages about the precise connection between the Wall Street Crash and the Great Depression of the 1930s – but basically, when people lose money they stop buying, so manufacturers stop producing and employers stop hiring people. So there was mass unemployment and bankruptcies in America, affecting virtually everybody in the country, with knock-on effects throughout the world.

The US banking system itself collapsed, leading to reforms in 1933 which separated the roles of commercial lending banks from those primarily involved in investment. The idea was that never again would greed and conflicts of interest be able to create the conditions for such a disastrous financial meltdown.

AT A GLANCE

The Wall Street Crash of 1929, in which share prices slumped due to panic selling by investors heralded the Great Depression, which afflicted the USA for most of the 1930s. Shares took a quarter of a century to regain their 1929 price levels, and the human cost – probably as long-lasting – was considerably greater.

Above: A bronze monument in Delhi commemorates Gandhi's 1930 Salt March to Dandi.

Left: Mahatma Gandhi , third from the left (head down), on his famous march to make salt, in defiance of the British monopoly.

GANDHI COMPLETES SALT MARCH

DANDI, INDIA

APRIL 5, 1930

Mohandas Karamchand Gandhi will be forever associated with India's fight for independence against the British Raj. He was instrumental in India's eventual victory, and his salt march to Dandi in 1930 was seen as the defining moment in the struggle. Known as Mahatma, 'great soul', Gandhi was India's spiritual leader and chief political activist during its battle for autonomy, and it was his philosophy and practice of *satyagraha* that was integral to the success of the salt march and to the defusing of the conflict that had been grumbling on for decades.

Satyagraha means non-violent action, primarily through civil resistance. Gandhi urged his followers, rather than becoming violent and rioting – thus making the problems worse – to quietly disobey the rules and stay true to their own principles.

He rejected claims that this was just passive resistance, stating that the goal of satyagraha was 'to convert, not to coerce, the wrong-doer'. For Gandhi, success was people helping their antagonists to discover the obstruction they have raised, so that everyone can work together to remove it and come to an amicable and mutually respectful resolution. This was his main tool in trying to remove the colonial authority of the British Raj over India.

He had already been imprisoned by the British for attempting to inspire insurrection in 1922, but a few years later he returned to the limelight, focusing on the Empire's new taxation laws on salt, which put this vital substance out of the reach of most Indians. He planned to march from his home in Sabarmati to Dandi, with the intention of producing his own salt. The 241-mile (390-km) trek drew worldwide press attention, and many Indians joined him on the way. He reached Dandi 26 days later, on April 5, 1930, reaching down to grasp his own symbolic handful of salt. Nationwide civil resistance followed, with millions of Indians producing their own salt or purchasing it tax-free. Over 60,000 were arrested, including Gandhi; the conflict went on for a year until agreement was reached: release of the prisoners for suspension of civil resistance.

This was a pivotal point in the long march towards independence, with the planet watching; the salt satyagraha of 1930 would become known as one of Gandhi's highest achievements. It wasn't, however, until 1946 that the salt tax laws were abolished, and a year later, in August 1947, that India finally became an independent nation.

Gandhi lived to see India's independence, but at a prayer meeting in New Delhi in 1948 he was assassinated by extremist Nathuram Godse. Gandhi had been one of the world's greatest modern thinkers, a man who had led his country to self-government by peaceful means.

AT A GLANCE

The example in civil resistance set by Mahatma Gandhi in 1930 in defying a tax on salt would sow the seeds that resulted in India receiving its independence from the British Empire in 1947. Salt, a commodity esential to all, was used as a metaphor for freedom, and both goals were achieved by non-violent means.

Above: Owens betters the Olympic record with his time of 21.1 seconds during a 200-meter heat.

Right: The start of the 100 meters at the 1936 Olympic Games in Berlin.

JESSE OWENS, OLYMPIC CHAMPION

BERLIN, GERMANY
AUGUST 3, 1936

When the Olympic Games was held in Germany in 1936, Adolf Hitler saw it as a chance to display a 'resurgent' country. In reality, Germany had a dark interior, tainted by scientific racism and the focus on the 'Aryan race' – but African-American athlete Jesse Owens upset the applecart when he won four gold medals, including the prestigious men's 100 meters.

The 22-year-old Owen had already set sprinting world records while a student at Ohio State University. But, as for many black people in America, life was far from easy for him; he lived in a segregated society, needed to work at multiple jobs to pay his way through college, and was denied a scholarship despite his athletic prowess.

For all the United States' racial problems, however, it was Germany who later came to the fore with its persecution of anyone who did not fit with Hitler's views for the country. But the Second World War was still three years away, and the Olympics had been awarded to Berlin five years before, in 1931. The world turned up to watch, albeit slightly apprehensively.

The USA had considered boycotting the games due to the already well publicized Nazi administration, but finally agreed to attend. Its argument that sport should not be bound up with politics and discrimination was justified, yet it was considered hypocritical coming from a country with its own racial problems. Berlin and the surrounding areas were 'cleaned up' in an attempt to allay the suspicions of the visitors; anti-Semitic propaganda was concealed, and any 'unwanted' natives were hidden in camps. Ironically, Owens whilst in the fascist country did not have to comply with segregation, enjoying the same rights as his white counterparts. He even became the first black man to receive sports sponsorship, when a young German businessman named Adi Dassler persuaded him to wear his Adidas footwear.

In the 100 meters, Owens fended off a late challenge from previous world record holder Ralph Metcalfe, to win the gold. During the next five days Owens won three more gold medals: in the long jump, the 200 meters and the men's relay.

Owens' achievement was a monumental one, and it seriously dented Hitler's vision of Aryan superiority. But amidst claims that Hitler had snubbed Owens at the games, Owens pointed out it was actually his own country that had slighted him; despite his achievements he heard nothing from President Roosevelt.

Owens returned to the USA a hero, but he got into financial difficulties, and when he pursued commercial opportunities his amateur status was rescinded. He died in 1980 aged 66, but his legacy lives on as the man who showed it is the individual, not nationality, creed or race, that defines a person.

AT A GLANCE

Black athlete Jesse Owens dominated the 1936 Olympic Games in Germany, winning four gold medals. Yet his achievement was all but ignored by the authorities in his native United States, where segregation was still rife – ironically, since the USA disapproved of Hitler's Aryan ideals.

R-1108

Above: Aerial View of Crude Oil Refinery.

Left: Two men view the site of the Arabian American Oil Company's first successful oil well in Saudi Arabia at Dharan.

LARGEST SUPPLY OF CRUDE OIL FOUND IN 20TH CENTURY

SAUDI ARABIA
MARCH 1938

Oil is the most actively traded commodity on the planet and has a huge impact on the world's economy. So when a huge supply of crude oil was found in Saudi Arabia it was very big news indeed.

Until the 1930s, the kingdom of Saudi Arabia had no real interest in oil; its economy had relied on pilgrimages to the holy sites of Mecca and Medina, the two most sacred cities in the Muslim religion of Islam. The kingdom had been created by Abd-al-Aziz ibn Saud in 1932 after he had spent three decades reclaiming the land he believed belonged to his family, the House of Saud.

The United States saw the untapped potential of newly formed Saudi Arabia's 830,000 square miles of land, and approached ibn Saud about the possibility of drilling for oil in what was now the largest country in the Middle East.

The King hoped they might find water, and so authorized giant company Standard Oil of California to explore a desert bordering the Persian Gulf, in the northeast of the country, in 1933. Four years of drilling yielded no results and it was beginning to look like a futile exercise until, in March 1938, the eastern province was chosen for the seventh attempt to discover oil. They struck more oil than had ever been seen in history.

What the Americans found would be called the Ghawar Field – 1.3 billion acres of crude oil spanning 173 miles. It is estimated that this oil field alone would account for more than half Saudi Arabia's oil production.

Six years later, the originally US-controlled oil company was renamed Arabian American Oil Company, commonly known as Aramco, and it was fully nationalized by the Saudis in 1980. Saudi Arabia had become the most oil-rich country on the planet, and as such held an incredible amount of bargaining power in the world's marketplace. Oil accounts for over 90 per cent of Saudi's exports; it is estimated to possess over 250 billion barrels in reserve, and still extracts 5 million barrels per day.

That day in March 1938 was the making of a country. No longer having to rely on tourism and pilgrimage to scrape an economy together, Saudi Arabia found itself winning the global equivalent of the lottery and becoming one of the most important nations in the world.

AT A GLANCE

The opportunism of the USA was the catalyst for the discovery, in 1938, of the largest supply of crude oil ever found, in the newly created country of Saudi Arabia. This country's ownership of the planet's most actively traded commodity made it, during most of the 20th century and the early part of the 21st, the most oil-rich country in the world, increasing exponentially both its political importance and its wealth.

Above: Nazi Panzer tanks forge through Belgium in May 1940, conquering the country in less than three weeks.

Right: German troops travel past Cleopatra's Needle in Paris, June 1940, following the Nazi invasion of France.

Below: Ju-87 Stuka dive-bombers helped push the Allies back from northern France to the Channel coas.t

NAZI BLITZKRIEG ON THE WESTERN FRONT

THE NETHERLANDS, BELGIUM, LUXEMBOURG, FRANCE

MAY 10, 1940

The Nazi invasion of Poland in September 1939 caused the United Kingdom and France to declare war on Germany. But during the first few months after that, the European nations held back – this period known as the Phoney War – waiting to see whether Adolf Hitler intended to conquer any more territories.

The answer came with his invasion of Norway and Denmark in April 1940. The Phoney War finally ended on May 10, when the Nazis launched Operation Yellow (*Fall Gelb*), the blitzkrieg against the Netherlands, Belgium and Luxembourg. Together with France, Norway and Denmark (and, later, Germany itself) the battle zones in these countries were known as the Western Front of World War II.

Blitzkrieg is German for 'lightning war' and its use took the Allies by surprise. Tanks advanced rapidly across open country, but the new dimension came from above, in the demoralizing and crippling bombing raids on major cities and supply points. The Nazis used these techniques rapidly and decisively, giving their enemies little chance to recover or strike back.

The blitzkrieg avoided the prolonged trench warfare of World War I. Also, the concept of highly mobile troops combined with aircraft had the advantage of not contravening the Treaty of Versailles, which had at the end of World War 1 strictly limited the size of the German army. Now, the Nazi advance, spearheaded by the immensely powerful Panzer Mark III tanks, sliced its way into the Netherlands, forcing its surrender within five days. Luxembourg held out for only 48 hours. The fall of Belgium took just 18 days.

The attack on the Low Countries was partly a diversionary tactic. Hitler's main target was France, and the invasion, code-named Operation Red (*Fall Rot*), began on May 13. German armored units pushed from Belgium through the densely forested Ardennes region before moving quickly towards the English Channel. The Allied forces, consisting of the British Expeditionary Force alongside French and Belgian troops, were overwhelmed. After an unsuccessful counterattack at Arras, the Allies were forced to retreat to Dunkirk, from where 338,226 soldiers were evacuated over a nine-day period between May 26 and June 4.

France fell to Germany within seven weeks, sending shockwaves around the world. An armistice was agreed on June 25, with most of France occupied, but part of the south remaining as the Free Zone. It was a stunning victory for Germany, achieving in less than two months what four years of trench warfare in World War I had failed to do.

AT A GLANCE

Learning from the lessons of World War I's stalemate trench warfare, Germany employed a combination of aerial bombing and highly mobile artillery to blaze a trail across Europe in 1940, causing the British army to retreat across the English Channel from Dunkirk. It would take the Allies four years to regain the lost ground and turn the tide of the war.

Above: Russian tanks roll towards the battle front on June 22, 1941, the first day of the German drive to defeat the USSR.

Right: Women dig anti-tank trenches near Moscow to confound Hitler's Operation Barbarossa.

OPERATION BARBAROSSA – HITLER INVADES RUSSIA

USSR
JUNE 22, 1941

The German offensive against the USSR, codenamed Operation (*Fall*) Barbarossa, was the largest military operation of all time, with more than 4.5 million troops invading along a 1,800-mile front, with 600,000 motor vehicles and 750,000 horses. The assault began on June 22, 1941.

Hitler intended to conquer Russia using the blitzkrieg technique which had been so successful on the Western Front. The Germans confidently expected that the USSR would fall as easily as France. The result of six months' detailed planning, Operation Barbarossa aimed to conquer the European part of the Soviet Union, up to the A–A line between the cities of Archangelsk and Astrakhan.

Although Hitler had long nurtured the ambition to invade the Soviet Union, his intentions had been masked by a non-aggression treaty, the Molotov–Ribbentrop Pact, signed shortly before Germany invaded Poland in 1939. This agreement had surprised the world because of the visible mutual hostility and the ideological differences between Germany and the USSR. A trade pact followed in 1940, but the two countries still remained suspicious of each other. The Soviet Union was invited to enter the Axis Pact with Germany, Italy and Japan, but negotiations broke down, making war between them more likely.

Hitler believed that the Russian Army was in a weakened state. Meanwhile, German propaganda claimed that Operation Barbarossa was a necessary pre-emptive strike against a dangerous foe. Then the German campaign in the Balkans spilt over into war with Russia. Yet, despite the massing of Axis troops on the border between German-controlled Romania and Russia during February 1941, the attack took the Soviets by surprise; the Russian leader, Stalin, had not believed that Germany would open up the war on a second front.

The Nazis made significant gains during the early part of the operation, capturing some important economic areas like the Ukraine – but they fatally underestimated the stoic endurance of the Soviet Red Army. The Nazis had been so confident they would secure victory before the onset of the harsh Russian winter that they had failed to prepare for it, and so the freezing weather and poor road conditions contributed to the ultimate failure of their campaign.

By October 1941 the Germans had got close to the Russian capital, but then they lost the two-month Battle of Moscow. The decisive moment arrived when a Red Army counterattack on December 5 forced the Nazis back and crippled Operation Barbarossa. But even so, the war on the Eastern Front continued, with the Germans attacking Stalingrad in 1942, and, at the northern end of the battle line, the siege of Leningrad which dragged on until 1944.

AT A GLANCE

Hitler's strike against Russia, Operation Barbarossa, in June 1941, opened a second front in the European war. But the combination of inhospitable Russian winter and terrain plus the opposing Red Army, on their home ground and used to the conditions, proved impossible for the Germans to overcome. When the Germans failed to take Moscow after a long-drawn-out battle, Barbarossa was doomed to failure.

F3

ATTACK ON PEARL HARBOR

HAWAII

DECEMBER 7, 1941

Until 9/11, it was December 7, 1941, that was the date no American alive at the time would ever forget. The Japanese attacks on the US naval base in the Hawaiian port of Pearl Harbor caused devastating casualties and propelled the United States into the Second World War.

Above: The battleship USS Arizona *sinks after being bombed by Japanese planes on December 7, 1941.*

Left: Sinking battleships after the Japanese bombing of Pearl Harbor include USS California *(right foreground) and* Oklahoma.

Inset: Mitsubishi dive-bombers on deck of a Japanese carrier before their attack on Pearl Harbor.

Tensions between the USA and Japan had been building for some time, escalating in the 1930s due to Japan's treatment of neighboring China. As a result of Japan's invasion of French Indochina at the turn of the 1940s, the USA cut its oil exports to Japan. This forced the Japanese to look for their supplies to Indonesia – at the time ruled by the Dutch – and to the US-owned Philippines.

As an attempt to invade the Philippines would obviously result in a strong US counterattack, the Japanese decided to immobilize the US forces before attempting to overrun the islands, and the nearest US base to the Philippines was Pearl Harbor.

Japan sent a message to the USA informing them of their intention to cease negotiations. This was due to arrive before the attack, but because of communication failures and decryption errors, the message did not arrive until after the attack had begun.

The attack came as a complete surprise to the USA; both countries had been well aware of the potential for conflict, but the USA had believed the Japanese would go after the Philippines first, and had underestimated the Japanese military strength. American radar had actually spotted the Japanese fleet – but had misidentified them, thinking they were friendly.

Just before 8 a.m. on Sunday December 7, the Japanese attacked, with an air raid lasting nearly two hours. The death toll reached over 2,300, half of that from the battleship USS *Arizona*, which was destroyed by a Japanese bomb just minutes into the assault.

With the harbor laid waste, seven US ships destroyed and more ships seriously damaged, the United States policy of isolationism from the war had to be re-assessed. The next day, President Roosevelt addressed the nation, and less than an hour later the USA declared war on Japan.

In 1945, German forces surrendered in May, and the war with Japan ended in August with the atomic bombs on Hiroshima and Nagasaki.

AT A GLANCE

Japan's undeclared air attack on Pearl Harbor impelled the USA into involvement in the Second World War, and so this was a pivotal moment in the conflict. Over 2,300 people were injured or killed there – but four years later Japan suffered the US nuclear attacks on Hiroshima and Nagasaki.

Overleaf: The battleships U.S.S. West Virginia (foreground) and U.S.S. Tennessee sit low in the water and burn after the Japanese surprise attack on Pearl Harbor.

GERMAN SURRENDER AT STALINGRAD

USSR
FEBRUARY 2, 1943

The Battle of Stalingrad was one of the bloodiest in history, with casualties estimated at more than 1.5 million. The battle involved more participants, military and civilian, than any other. The levels of bloodshed and brutality were unparalleled. The decisive victory it gave Russia, however, marked a major turning point in World War II, with the German army suffering its first major military setback. It was the start of the Soviet counter-offensive which contributed to Germany's unconditional surrender in 1945.

Above: The battered city of Stalingrad as it looked during its siege by German forces in 1942 and 1943.

Left: Prisoners are marched through the snowy streets of Stalingrad after the German defeat by Soviet forces in February 1943.

Inset: A huge World War II memorial to the defenders of Stalingrad on Mamayev Hill, scene of some of the fiercest fighting.

After being repulsed from Moscow in December 1941, the German army regrouped and waited until spring 1942, when they would not be hindered by the severe winter weather, to launch their second offensive in Russia. Capturing Stalingrad was important to Hitler because it was a major industrial centre whose location on the Volga river was vital for transportation. If the Nazis controlled Stalingrad, they could cut off the fuel supplies to the Russian military – and Hitler relished the propaganda coup that would come from seizing the city named after Stalin, the Soviet leader.

The German army began its push into southern Russia on June 28, 1942, meeting little opposition at first, and reaching the outskirts of Stalingrad by the end of July. Stalin, well aware of the crucial nature of the battle, ordered that anyone capable of holding a rifle should do so, and the Russians took him at his word, and prepared to defend their city at all costs.

The Luftwaffe's bombing reduced much of Stalingrad to rubble. German troops gained control of up to 90 per cent of the city from time to time, but they were never able to eradicate the last pockets of resistance in the city center, on the west bank of the Volga; the Germans were better at coordinated, combined mass assaults than the hand-to-hand, house-to-house skirmishing which they faced in Stalingrad. The fighting dragged on for months, into the same bitter Russian winter conditions had already defeated the Nazis, earlier that same year.

Taking advantage of this, Stalin launched a counter-attack, codenamed Operation Uranus (Операция Уран), in November 1942. A pincer movement, it trapped the Nazi troops inside the city, cutting them off from their supplies. Besieged for three bitter months and unable to break out, the surviving Germans, starving, frozen and desperate, surrendered in February 1943. In doing this their commander, Field Marshal von Paulus, had disobeyed Hitler's order to fight to the last man and take his own life rather than be captured, and so he incurred Hitler's wrath. It was from this point on that the army generals started to lose confidence in Hitler.

AT A GLANCE

Germany's failure to hold the vital industrial centre of Stalingrad would prove the turning point in the second front against Russia, opened two years earlier in 1941. Despite occupying the city, the Germans were unable to overcome spirited and tenacious Russian resistance, and the Germans' eventual surrender came as a body blow to Hitler's reputation and ambition.

D-DAY LANDINGS TURN THE TIDE OF WAR

NORMANDY, FRANCE
JUNE 6, 1944

Above: Omaha Beach pictured on D-Day as Allied forces made landfall and the tide of war in Europe turned irrevocably.

Right: American troops disembark on one of the Normandy invasion beaches on June 7, 1944, the day after D-Day.

Below: General Dwight D Eisenhower (left) confers with his deputy, Britain's Field Marshal Bernard Montgomery (right).

AT A GLANCE

Codenamed Operation Overlord, the Allied landings in northern France in June 1944 signaled the beginning of the last phase of the war in Europe. After the landings, British, US and Canadian forces pushed towards Paris and then towards the Netherlands: Russian forces moved in from the east, and Hitler's days were numbered.

World War II in Europe entered its final phase with the landing of Allied troops in German-occupied France. Beginning in the early hours of June 6, 1944, Operation Overlord was masterminded by US General Dwight D. Eisenhower (Ike), as Supreme Commander of the Allied Expeditionary Force. The Allied forces were composed of British, US and Canadian units together with representatives of the Free French. Known as the 21st Army Group, they were commanded by Field Marshal Viscount Montgomery of Alamein (Monty), the British general famous for his victory at El Alamein in Egypt in 1942.

After a day's delay because of bad weather, the landings took place along a 50-mile strip on the coast of Normandy. This comprised five beaches, codenamed Gold, Sword, Juno, Omaha and Utah. There were two phases to the assault, starting with an air attack shortly after midnight followed by an amphibious landing at 6.30 a.m.

The invading force was massive, consisting of some 5,000 ships and 13,000 aircraft from the United States Air Force alone. Two temporary harbors, known as Mulberries, were constructed for use until the existing harbors could be captured. During the first day of the operation, 175,000 Allied personnel went ashore.

German resistance was determined, particularly on Omaha and Utah, the beaches attacked by the US troops. But the Allied forces soon established a beachhead, supported by airborne assaults using paratroopers and glider-borne soldiers. From there, they gradually fanned out into the French countryside. During the fighting, the Allies sustained approximately 10,000 casualties, whilst it is estimated that the Germans suffered up to 9,000.

Within four weeks, more than a million Allied troops had landed in Normandy, and the German army was pushed back towards the River Seine. Some 100,000 Germans surrendered at Falaise. Then, with the invasion of southern France, victory for the Allies grew closer.

Paris was liberated in late August, and the Allies moved towards the Netherlands and the Rhine Valley, although they suffered occasional setbacks such as the failure to capture the bridges at Arnhem in Holland. When the Germans counterattack was repulsed at the Battle of the Bulge, the Nazis' last hope of success on the Western Front had gone.

With the Russians advancing from the east, the war was nearly over. American and Russian forces converged on the banks of the River Elbe, and two days later, on April 30, 1945, Hitler committed suicide in his bunker in Berlin. The Germans surrendered unconditionally on May 7, 1945, and the war in Europe was over.

US

Above: Colonel Paul W Tibbets stands next to the Boeing B-29 he piloted on its historic bombing mission over Hiroshima.

Left: A mushroom cloud rises over Nagasaki on August 9, 1945, as the USA drops a second atomic bomb. Japan surrendered five days later, ending the war.

Inset: Only a few buildings were left standing in Hiroshima after the destruction wrought by the US atomic bomb.

ATOM BOMB DROPPED

HIROSHIMA, JAPAN

AUGUST 6, 1945

The Second World War had raged for six years, the death tolls for the countries involved running into tens of millions. The planet had never seen such death and destruction, but in 1945 it appeared an end was in sight. On August 6, the USA dropped the world's first atomic bomb on the Japanese city of Hiroshima.

The Allies had won the battle against the Axis countries of Germany and Italy, which were imploding: Italy had surrendered in 1943, and Germany had signed an unconditional surrender early in 1945, ending the war in Europe. But Japan refused to give up.

During the war the USA had begun the top secret Manhattan Project, aimed at equipping the country with nuclear weapons. Born out of the fear that Nazi Germany was doing the same, the project began on a small scale but quickly escalated into a major industry, employing over 100,000, people including some of the foremost scientists on the planet.

On July 16, 1945, they tested the first atom bomb in Los Alamos, New Mexico – the same day as US President Harry Truman, Britain's Winston Churchill and the Soviet Union leader Josef Stalin met in Potsdam to discuss the fate of a defeated Germany. The three leaders ordered the surrender of Japan, threatening 'utter destruction' if the Japanese did not comply. Japan ignored the ultimatum.

At 8.15 a.m. on August 6, the Enola Gay, a B-29 Superfortress bomber aircraft, dropped the world's first atomic bomb onto humans, in Hiroshima. Picked for its importance as an army depot, the city was obliterated in a giant mushroom cloud of smoke, an image that would go down in history.

The bomb had 2,000 times more power than any other explosive ever used in the war, and killed a reported 166,000 people, the majority of them civilians. Those who did not die from the original blast perished from flash burns or radiation sickness, which affected many in the city for years after. The immediate blast radius was one square mile, with flash fires ravaging a further four.

Just three days later the US dropped a second bomb, this time on Nagasaki, a strategic Japanese port. The city was completely destroyed, with another 80,000 deaths.

With two vital cities wiped out and the threat of more atom bomb attacks, Japan surrendered unconditionally five days later, on August 14, although the document was not signed until September 2. The war was over, but peace had come at an appalling cost; the world now knew of a weapon so powerful that it could destroy all human and animal life on the planet.

AT A GLANCE

With Italy and Germany defeated, the Allies decided on nuclear bombing to end Japanese resistance and win the Second World War in 1945. Hiroshima and Nagasaki were the cities chosen for the strikes that ended that conflict – but which also started the Cold War between the West and Russia, who both had the atomic might to destroy humanity.

PARTITION OF INDIA

INDIA/PAKISTAN
AUGUST 15, 1947

India had been governed by Britain since 1612, originally by the British East India Company, and after 1858 as a British colony. At that time, India was made up of a number of large provinces directly administered by the British, together with over 500 princely states which the British ruled indirectly through their Indian sovereigns, who had sworn allegiance to Britain.

Above: Viceroy of India Lord Mountbatten meets with various Indian leaders to devise a plan to partition the country.

Right: Prime Minister Nehru addresses a mass meeting of Hindus and Muslims in Delhi in a plea to end fighting, October 1947.

Below: The border city of Amritsar was a main crossing point for people migrating between India and Pakistan.

Early in the 20th century, the country's largest political party, the Indian National Congress, had launched the struggle for a free state. India's spiritual and political leader, Mahatma Gandhi, was an advocate of independence, believing in non-violent opposition to British rule – but he was opposed to partition. The INC party leader, Jawaharlal Nehru, was also a key figure in the independence movement, and went on to become independent India's first Prime Minister.

In 1906, the All India Muslim League had been formed as a new political party by Muslims dissatisfied by the Hindu domination of the Indian National Congress. At the party's convention in 1930, writer/philosopher Allama Iqbal had proposed a separate region for Muslims, and although the party's president, Muhammad Ali Jinnah, had initially favored a united India, by 1935 he had become convinced that division on religious lines was necessary.

In January 1946, after a series of mutinies amongst British Indian forces, bloody Hindu/Muslim riots broke out in Calcutta (now Kolkata) and spread throughout the country. These events spurred Britain's new Labour government into action. Deciding that Britain could no longer control India, the prime minister, Clement Attlee, announced that independence was to be granted and the country was to be divided.

The newly-appointed viceroy of India, Lord Mountbatten, was given the task of drawing up the map of a partitioned India. Under the Mountbatten Plan, the predominantly Hindu and Sikh areas formed the new India, whilst areas with a Muslim majority comprised Pakistan. The latter was split into East and West, separated geographically by India, and the princely states were allowed to decide which country to join. In the following months, millions of refugees migrated across the newly-drawn borders, resulting in scenes of unprecedented violence and the loss of about half a million lives.

The Indo–Pakistani War of 1947 was fought over the former princely state of Jammu and Kashmir, which had a Hindu leader but a Muslim majority. This war was the first of four post-partition conflicts, three of which were over Kashmir; the last conflict, in 1971, saw East Pakistan become the independent nation of Bangladesh.

AT A GLANCE

When Britain granted India independence on August 15, 1947, the process also led to the foundation of Pakistan. This new country was formed from the two principal Muslim regions, in the east and the west, with the remaining territory still belonging to India – mainly Hindu and Sikh – separating them. This untidy compromise was followed, in 1971, by East Pakistan becoming the independent nation of Bangladesh.

FIRST FASTER THAN SOUND FLIGHT

CALIFORNIA, USA
OCTOBER 14, 1947

AT A GLANCE

The prestige of breaking the sound barrier in a manned aircraft went to Chuck Yeager in 1947. So the combat warplanes of the 1950s and beyond went supersonic, and were powered by turbojets rather than rockets – but during the rest of the 20th century it was only a single commercial aircraft, Concorde, that was able to bring the benefit of these speeds to civil aviation.

In the aftermath of the atomic bomb, the United States continued their mission to be the most pioneering and innovative country on the planet. On October 14, 1947, they flew the first aircraft to break the sound barrier.

Left: Charles E. Yeager, Major Gus Lundquist and Captain James Fitzgerald (left to right), stand before the XS-1 at Muroc Air Force Base, California.

Below: President Truman awards the Collier Air Trophy, aviation's highest honor, to scientist John Stack, Chuck Yeager and Lawrence D. Bell, president of Bell Aircraft Corporation.

It had all begun in March 1945, five months before the obliteration of Hiroshima and Nagasaki. The National Advisory Committee for Aeronautics – which later, as NASA, became the organization that sent men to the moon – commissioned three aircraft titled XS-1 (experimental supersonic) to gather information about transonic and supersonic flight.

Abbreviated to X-1, the aircraft looked more like a machine-gun bullet than an airplane, and first took to the skies via gliding flights in January 1946. The first powered flight was by Chalmers Goodlin towards the end of the year, but he was removed from the program after his wage demands and calls for hazard pay were deemed to be excessive.

Enter Charles 'Chuck' Yeager; under the new control of the United States Air Force, World War Two pilot Yeager was selected as the new pilot of the X-1 project. He named the aircraft Glamorous Glennis after his wife who he had wed in February 1945.

The 23-year-old nearly dropped out of his historic flight that day. A horse-riding accident had left him with broken ribs, but he persevered despite being in so much pain that he could barely walk. Yeager later said, "If it became physically impossible to climb into the X-1, then I'd scrub the mission. If I could get into the pilot's seat, I knew I could fly."

Get in the cockpit he did, and the X-1 was launched from a B-29 bomber over California in an eerie comparison with the atomic bombings two years previously. The rocket aircraft was the first to reach supersonic speeds, recorded at Mach 1.06 – 807 mph.

According to Yeager, he travelled faster than sound for 18 seconds. He reflected on the event and its significance for the USA, saying: "It opened up space for us and put us ahead of the rest of the world in aeronautical knowledge."

It was another race won for the USA, both figuratively and literally. The USA would go on to record many more achievements, the highlight undoubtedly landing men on the moon. But for now they could be content with being the fastest nation in the world.

Above: Members of the newly created state of Israel gather to hear Prime Minister David Ben-Gurion read the Declaration of Independence.

Left: Arab soldiers shell Jewish forces striving to recapture the vital supply route from Tel Aviv to Jerusalem.

STATE OF ISRAEL IS PROCLAIMED

TEL AVIV, ISRAEL
MAY 14, 1948

Zionism, the movement calling for an independent Jewish state, gained momentum in the late 19th century, with a wave of Russian Jews migrating to their traditional homelands in Palestine. After the collapse of the Ottoman Empire in 1917, Britain took control of the region, and the British Prime Minister Balfour lent his support to the idea; but Arab objections during the 1920s and 1930s stalled moves to create the state.

At the end of the Second World War, the revelations about the Holocaust aroused greater international sympathy for the cause. But the Arabs remained violently opposed to the proposed partition of Palestine, a country in which they had been for many centuries the majority and saw as their own. Britain went to the newly formed United Nations, which ruled in favor of the division of the country.

Britain, whose mandate to rule in the area was due to expire on May 15, 1948, refused to implement the new scheme. It regarded the UN solution as unworkable, since the majority Palestinian population was to be left only 46 per cent of the original territory. But the Jewish settlers took up arms, and seized control of the area assigned to them; on the eve of the departure of the British, the Jewish leader, David Ben-Gurion, proclaimed the new state of Israel in a ceremony in Tel Aviv's Art Museum.

As the British marched out of Israel, forces from Egypt, Jordan, Syria, Lebanon and Iraq invaded it in support of the Palestinians. But the Jews of Israel not only defended themselves but seized further territory, expanding Israel's original borders by 50 per cent. The fighting ended in 1949 when the UN sanctioned this expansion; hundreds of thousands of Palestinians fled their homes, becoming refugees in the remnants of Palestine controlled by Jordan and Egypt.

After the Second World War, many people had seen the creation of a separate Jewish state as a moral imperative. But imposing a minority Jewish population from outside onto the long-settled Arab people of the area was always going to create problems, and not just in the region itself. For example, the strong US support for Israel (declared by President Truman only 11 minutes after Ben-Gurion's proclamation) drew the USSR into opposition as suppliers of armaments to the Arab League.

Israel further increased its territory during the Six Day War in 1967 and established military supremacy in the region. But in the early years of the 21st century, despite peace agreements with Egypt in 1979 and the Palestine Liberation Organization in 1993, Israel's existence continues to trigger acts of war and terrorism both within and beyond the Palestinian homelands.

AT A GLANCE

The division of Jews and Arabs into the states of Palestine and Israel proved controversial in 1948 and remains so today. The bid to expand Israel's borders won UN approval, but subsequent peace agreements have failed to suppress both resentment and terrorist acts.

Left: German police and American soldiers face Soviet soldiers at the border between Allied- and Soviet-controlled Berlin in 1948.

Right: Residents of Berlin wave to an American airlift plane approaching Tempelhof Airfield.

BERLIN BLOCKADE BEGINS

EAST GERMANY

JUNE 24, 1948

At the end of the Second World War the Allies (France, Britain, United States and Soviet Union) occupied the defeated Germany and divided the entire country, and its capital, Berlin, into four administrative zones. The four powers were united in wanting to ensure that Germany's military capacity and ambitions could not be revived, but they disagreed about the role the country should have in post-war Europe.

The Western Allies wanted Germany to be fully integrated into Western Europe, so that, as they said, they could 'keep a watchful eye' on it. The Soviet Union was, however, concerned that a country so strongly supported by the capitalist West might destabilize the communist bloc in eastern Europe. Soviet leader Josef Stalin felt sure, too, that the US recovery program for Europe, the Marshall Plan, was a ploy to disguise a Western attempt to infiltrate his post-war buffer zone of communist states in eastern Europe, so he did not go to the European talks in early 1948 which resulted in the formation of West Germany.

Berlin was located deep in the Soviet sector of Germany, through which all supplies for the city had to be transported. Stalin saw the city as a bargaining chip in his political ambitions; so overnight on June 23–24, the Soviet Union blocked all road, rail and river routes into and out of the city. Without deliveries, the 2.5 million inhabitants of West Berlin had food for only five weeks.

The Western Allies were taken by surprise. The USA recommended a show of military strength – which might have provoked a new war – but British Foreign Minister Ernest Bevin successfully argued for an airlift into the city. Part of the post-war settlement of Berlin had been the allocation to the Western Allies of three air corridors between West Germany and Berlin, and Bevin reasoned that the Soviets would not dare shoot down planes on a humanitarian mission.

From haphazard beginnings, the airlift became a visible demonstration of the West's political determination, industrial capacity and military co-ordination. At its height, up to 1,000 planes were airborne at any given time, one landing in West Berlin every three minutes, delivering 8,000 tons of freight a day.

The blockade was the first skirmish in the Cold War; its imposition led to the formation of NATO in April 1949, and alerted Europe to the potential threat of a powerful USSR. Meanwhile Stalin, thwarted, was forced to lift the blockade on May 12. And Germany remained divided, the dividing line forming part of the new Iron Curtain across Europe, until the fall of communism led to the country's reunification in 1990.

AT A GLANCE

When the Soviet Union attempted to isolate the city of Berlin, deep in East Germany, from Western supplies in 1948, the response of France, Britain and the United States was to supply the former German capital by air. Stalin's aggressive stance failed to intimidate the Allies, and Berlin, like Germany itself, remained divided between East and West for another 42 years.

Blume
BAHNHOF

Above: The United Nations General Assembly commemorated the 30th anniversary of the Universal Declaration of Human Rights in 1978.

Right: Eleanor Roosevelt, René Cassin and RSS Gunawardene celebrate the tenth anniversary of the Universal Declaration of Human Rights.

UNIVERSAL DECLARATION OF HUMAN RIGHTS ADOPTED

PALAIS DE CHAILLOT, PARIS, FRANCE

DECEMBER 10, 1948

Having just witnessed a second devastating world war, the United Nations General Assembly, established in 1945, adopted the Universal Declaration of Human Rights (UDHR) in 1948 as an attempt to outlaw oppression and discrimination. The document set down in writing for the first time a recognition by the international community that individual human rights and fundamental freedoms applied to everyone.

Pressure for such a bill of rights had been growing during the course of the war. In his 1941 State of the Union address, US President Franklin D. Roosevelt had called for the protection of what he termed the 'essential Four Freedoms': freedom of speech, freedom of conscience, freedom from fear and freedom from want. This became the slogan of a movement that sought to make human rights part of the conditions for peace at the end of the war. And after Roosevelt died in 1945, his widow Eleanor played a major role in fulfilling his vision.

The Universal Declaration had to reflect in its 30 articles the different values and traditions of the 58 member states of the United Nations. It was a common statement of mutual aspirations, a shared vision of a more equitable and just world. Its success is reflected by its virtually universal acceptance, and the Universal Declaration is today the best known human rights document in the world, having been translated into nearly 250 languages. It also serves as a model for numerous international treaties and declarations, and is incorporated in the constitutions and laws of many countries.

The text was drafted in just under two years from January 1947 by an eight-member drafting committee. This was chaired by Eleanor Roosevelt and included John Peters Humphrey (Canada), René Cassin (France), P.C Chang (China) and Charles Malik (Lebanon). They revised the draft declaration in the light of replies from member states before submitting it to the General Assembly. It was unanimously adopted, apart from eight abstentions, on December 10th, a date since celebrated annually as Human Rights Day.

For the first time in history, the international community had embraced a document considered to have universal value – 'a common standard of achievement for all peoples and all nations'. In 1966 the General Assembly also adopted two detailed covenants which complete the International Bill of Human Rights.

AT A GLANCE

The Universal Declaration of Human Rights arose directly from the horrors of World War II and is the first global expression of rights to which it is considered all people are entitled. Its 30 articles have since been elaborated in international treaties, regional human rights instruments and national constitutions and laws.

In
Your
Hands
A GUIDE FOR
COMMUNITY
ACTION

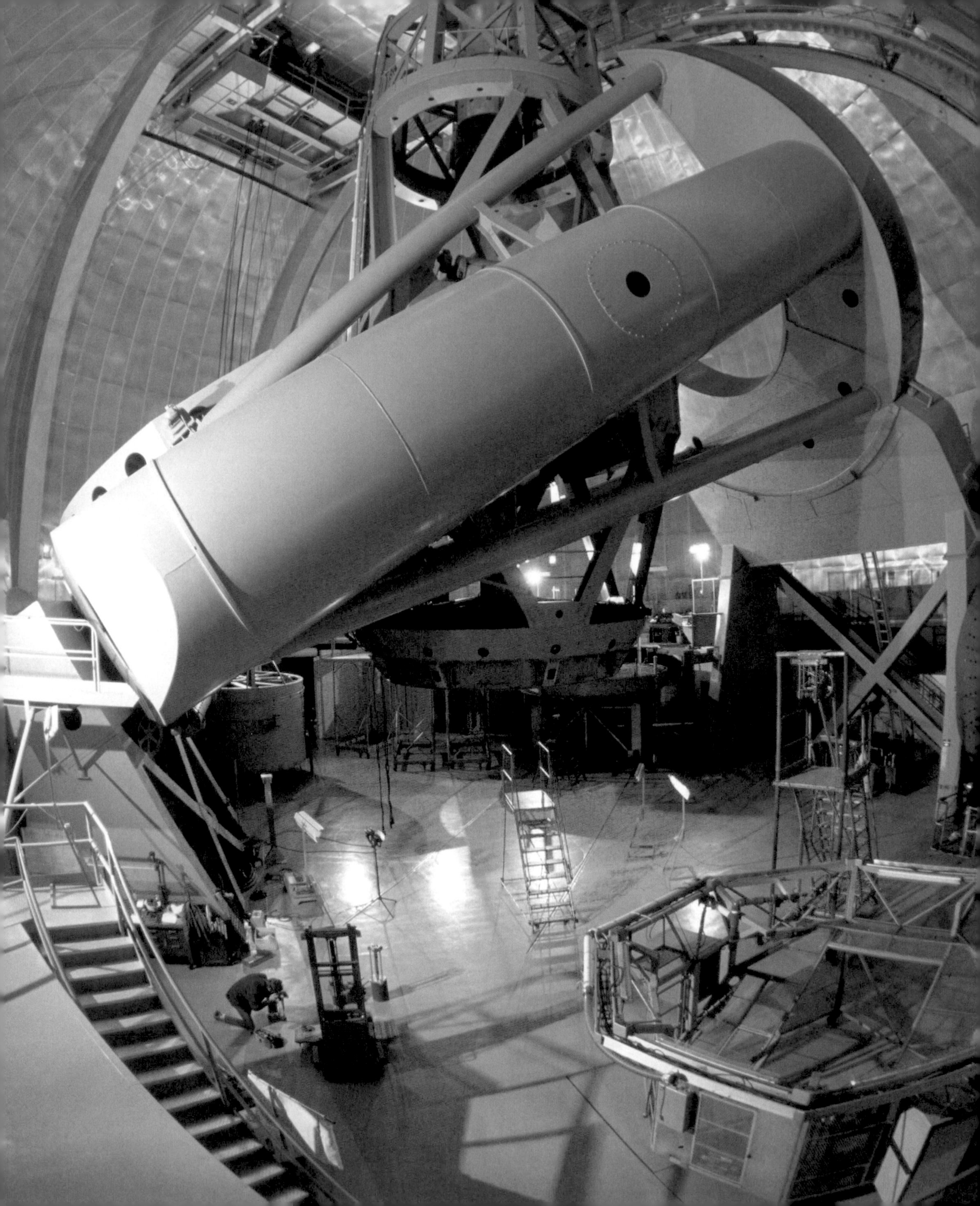

Above: Philip Staples (left), President of the Franklin Institute, presents the Franklin medal to Edwin Hubble in 1939.

Left: The Hale Telescope inside the Palomar Observatory, San Diego County, California.

HUBBLE FIRST USES THE HALE TELESCOPE

PALOMAR MOUNTAIN, USA

JANUARY 26, 1949

The Hale Telescope on Palomar Mountain was the last in a series of giant advances in telescope design by American astronomer George Ellery Hale. He had already founded observatories at Yerkes in Wisconsin and at Mount Wilson outside Los Angeles, both of which had made great improvements to the way space was observed from Earth.

At Mount Wilson, Hale had designed a 60-inch reflector telescope (an earlier Hale Telescope) which 'saw first light' (was first used for observation) in 1908. It was the largest telescope in the world until Hale built a second one nearby, the 100-inch Hooker Telescope. This saw first light in 1917, and it remained unsurpassed in size and quality for 30 years.

In 1919 Hale appointed Edwin Hubble to the staff at Mount Wilson, and Hubble's observations there of what became known as the Red Shift – the light-borne Doppler Effect produced by the rapid retreat of distant galaxies – provided firm evidence that the universe is expanding. His discovery, in 1929, became known as Hubble's Law, and it confirmed Lemaître's 'primeval atom' theory of 1927, later renamed the Big Bang.

Meanwhile, by 1928 it had become clear that they were going to need a bigger telescope. Hale won $6 million of funding from the Rockefeller Institute for a new telescope with a massive 200-inch reflector. The giant mirrored-glass parabolic bowl was made of Pyrex, a new material at the time, and innovative solutions were required not only for its manufacture but also for the support of this immensely heavy piece of equipment.

The original reflector bowl weighed 20 tons. Grinding and polishing it accurately (to within 2 nanometers) took 13 years and reduced its weight by five tons. The 1930 technique devised to coat the Pyrex in mirroring is still used today when it is periodically resurfaced.

The construction of the Hale Telescope at Palomar spanned major world events including the Great Depression and the Second World War. Hale, dying in 1938, did not live to see his greatest work come into service; it saw first light on January 26, 1949, when Hubble used it to make observations of a nebula, now known as Hubble's Variable Nebula, which he had first studied through the telescopes at Yerkes and Mount Wilson.

The Hale Telescope remained the largest telescope in the world for 27 years, and its high resolution was unbeaten until 1993. It was vital in studying the nature of quasars, and it is still a key research instrument for astronomers. Hubble's work with it was honored in the naming of the Hubble Space Telescope.

AT A GLANCE

The work of American astronomer George Ellery Hale and his protégé Edwin Hubble added much to our understanding of the universe around us. The Hale Telescope, inaugurated by Hubble in 1949, was the largest telescope in the world for 27 years and is still in use today.

BATTLE OF INCHON

SOUTH KOREA
SEPTEMBER 15, 1950

In June 1950, a series of skirmishes along the 38th parallel in partitioned Korea erupted into a full invasion. The North Korean People's Army (NKPA) raced southwards, catching South Korea off guard and capturing its capital, Seoul, after only three days before pressing on to the key south-eastern port of Pusan.

Above: Captured North Korean prisoners are marched at gunpoint after Inchon was secured by the USA.

Right: Smoke rises from shelled buildings in Inchon after the US bombardment.

Below: General Douglas MacArthur accompanies US troops during their attack on Inchon, September 1950.

A rearguard action by hurriedly assembled United Nations forces (chiefly from Britain, Australia and America) delayed the invading army and stopped them at the Pusan peninsula, the only part of South Korea never to fall under communist control. US General Douglas MacArthur secured the port, then conceived a daring counter-attack.

Inchon, a large port north-west of Seoul, had a well-protected harbor and was heavily defended by the NKPA. It was the last place they would expect a massive amphibious landing – so on September 15 this MacArthur masterstroke, led by the US Marines, took the communists completely by surprise.

The US forces took Inchon with minimum loss of life, cutting North Korean supply and communications lines and triggering a chaotic retreat. The liberation of Seoul was a much harder and bloodier battle, but with the enemy in disarray MacArthur was able to pursue them almost to the Chinese border in the far north of the country. But there, he in turn was caught out, unprepared for the massive intervention by the Chinese Army supporting the North Koreans.

Now it was the UN forces that retreated in disorder, to positions south of Seoul. But by the end of April 1951 they had fought their way back to a line more or less along the 38th parallel, where it had all begun. Two years of virtual stalemate followed whilst an armistice was discussed. It came into force in July 1953, when a demilitarized zone between the two countries was established, but peace in Korea has never been formally declared.

The decisiveness of the Battle of Inchon was a rare occasion in a brutal war which saw great loss of life (an estimated four million military and civilian) and achieved almost nothing. The war itself was the result of an unwelcome, arbitrary and unilateral division of Korea imposed by a joint US/Soviet committee onto the formerly Japanese territory. Having been separated, each side sought reunification on its own terms, and the USA was drawn into the conflict by its over-riding post-war foreign policy of containing the spread of communism at all costs. The Vietnam War was just around the corner.

AT A GLANCE

In the brief, bloody Korean War, the USA strove to stem the spread of communism by whatever means necessary. It was the precursor to a longer and even more costly conflict in Vietnam. The Korean War achieved nothing, either territorially or ideologically, and peace has never formally been declared.

DISCOVERY OF THE STRUCTURE OF DNA

CAMBRIDGE AND LONDON, UK
FEBRUARY 21, 1953

Above: Dr Francis Crick (left) and Dr James Watson (right) at a Molecular Biology Symposium.

Left: A computer-generated image of a strand of DNA.

It has long been understood that physical characteristics are passed on from generation to generation. Recognizing which gene is responsible for which trait has become the holy grail of the life sciences in the early 21st century. If genes are the building blocks of life, then deoxyribonucleic acid, DNA, is the instruction manual for assembling those blocks.

It's a relatively simple molecule, compared for example to protein, the other component of our life-defining chromosomes; DNA has only four sub-groups compared to protein's 20. Discovering how those sub-groups are structured was a vital first step in unlocking the genetic codes contained within them.

In the early 1950s, two teams of British scientists were racing to solve that problem. At Imperial College, London, Rosalind Franklin and Maurice Wilkins found a way to photograph DNA using X-ray diffraction. One image they produced clearly showed a spiral structure, a helix. Based on this visual evidence and on data about DNA established by many independent researchers, Francis Crick and James Watson of Cambridge University set about building a theoretical structure for the molecule.

Using metal rods and balls, they produced a model in the form of two intertwined, interconnected spirals, a double helix which satisfied all the known information about DNA. Crick and Watson announced their discovery on February 28, 1953, a week after they had completed their model. A month later, articles by Franklin, Wilkins, Crick and Watson appeared side by side in the influential science journal *Nature*.

Subsequent experiments confirmed the truth of Crick and Watson's theoretical model, and in 1962 Crick, Watson and Wilkins received a Nobel Prize for their discovery. Only living scientists are eligible for the prize, and Franklin had died in 1958; but neither Crick nor Watson cited her ground-breaking work in their Nobel lectures. Only Maurice Wilkins acknowledged her contribution.

With the structure of DNA established, all efforts turned to cracking the genetic code itself. Once that had been achieved, scientists set about mapping the genome, first in fruit flies (which have only 8 pairs of chromosomes) and eventually in humans (who have 46).

The discovery of the structure of DNA has led to significant insights into the development of species and indeed of life itself, and to an understanding and potential cure for genetic disorders. DNA forensics is now routinely applied to solving crimes. But with the benefits come ethical risks, and society is still wrestling with the moral dilemmas posed by our ability to engineer both animal and vegetable species genetically.

AT A GLANCE

The genetic code represented by DNA, discovered in 1953 by a group of British scientists, has revolutionized various aspects of life from solving crime to changing the characteristics of living creatures. Some believe it has also opened an ethical Pandora's box that may never be closed.

Above: Tenzing Norgay (left) and Edmund Hillary pose triumphantly at their camp after their return from the peak.

Left: Mount Everest as seen from the Rongbuk Monastery in China.

CONQUEST OF EVEREST

NEPAL/TIBET BORDER

MAY 29, 1953

It was only in 1856 that Peak XV, as it was then known to Westerners, was confirmed as the world's highest mountain. That year, calculations by the staff of Andrew Waugh, the British Surveyor General in India, proved that it was higher than the previous title holder, Kangchenjunga. The announcement had been delayed for four years while the team checked and rechecked their sums.

Although it was the policy of the Survey to retain local names wherever possible, Waugh never discovered this mountain's traditional names, Chomolungma and Sagarmatha, because Nepal and Tibet were at the time closed to Westerners – Waugh's staff had been carrying out their observations from a distance of more than 170 miles. So he named it after George Everest, his predecessor as Surveyor General. George Everest pointed out that his name could not be written in Hindi or pronounced by the local population; nevertheless in 1865 the British Geological Society formally adopted Mount Everest as the name of the world's highest place. Its generally accepted height, 8,848 m (29,029 ft) includes a 3.5 m (11 ft) allowance for snow and ice.

The first known expedition to the mountain was led by George Mallory in 1921. He aimed to explore the region for possible routes to the summit, and returned in 1924 for a serious assault. It was Mallory who, when asked why he was so intent on climbing Everest, replied, "Because it's there." He died in the attempt that year. His body was recovered 75 years later, but debate still rages about whether or not he had reached the summit before he died.

Other early attempts included a flight over Everest in 1933 by two Westland Wallace biplanes in an effort to drop a British flag onto the summit. It was funded by Lady Lucy Houston, an eccentric millionaire and former chorus girl.

The expedition led by John Hunt in 1953 was the ninth British outing. Hunt nominated two pairs of climbers from his team to make the final assault. The first pair were defeated by exhaustion just 100 m (300 ft) from the top. But at 11.30 a.m. on May 29, the second pair, New Zealander Edmund Hillary and Nepali Sherpa Tenzing Norgay, stepped onto the summit of Mount Everest and into the record books. They buried some sweets and a cross in the snow, took a few photos and came home.

News of the achievement reached Britain on the morning of Queen Elizabeth II's coronation. She promptly knighted Hunt and Hillary, and awarded the George Medal to Tenzing – and Tenzing, who did not know the date of his birth, adopted May 29 for all his subsequent birthdays.

AT A GLANCE

The conquering of Everest in 1953, then known as the world's highest peak, by Tenzing and Hillary is still, over half a century later, the most famous mountaineering feat in history. The fact that it coincided with Queen Elizabeth's coronation cemented it in history as a great British achievement that brightened up the drab postwar years, and in many people's minds heralded a new and great Elizabethan era.

Above: Senator Joseph R. McCarthy replies to Ed Murrow's televised attack, April 1954.

Right: Journalist Ed Murrow on the set of See It Now, *his television program which was aired on CBS from 1951 to 1958.*

EDWARD MURROW ATTACKS SENATOR JOSEPH McCARTHY

CBS TELEVISION NETWORK, USA
MARCH 9, 1954

In the immediate post-war years, American foreign policy was dominated by a single over-riding concern – to stop the spread of communism. Amongst most ordinary Americans, an atmosphere of concern and suspicion gradually deteriorated into one of intolerance and fear. For a few years it seemed that America's sense of liberty and justice had been lost in a blind panic; and that panic was encouraged and exploited by Edgar Hoover, director of the FBI, together with a junior Republican senator from Wisconsin, Joseph McCarthy.

The FBI's role in this panic was covert, and so it was the senator who gave his name to its public face: McCarthyism. Employees, particularly in government, education and the media, were rigorously interrogated, sacked on the merest whiff of sympathy with communism, blacklisted, and encouraged to give up the names of other supposed communist sympathizers. There was some evidence of communist infiltration ... but the McCarthy witch-hunt destroyed the lives and careers of many innocent people and their families. The invasive mistrust of colleagues had more in common with the secret police society of East Germany than with the Land of the Free.

Although most of America was swept up in the hysteria, there were resisting voices. Edward Murrow was a respected television journalist who had made his name with radio broadcasts to America from Europe during the Second World War. He had a reputation for fair and honest reporting, and he ran a weekly 30-minute slot called *See It Now* on the US television channel CBS. A 1953 edition of the program had exposed unfair McCarthyist dismissals within the air force. Expecting that McCarthy would now turn his guns his way, Murrow decided to devote his broadcast of March 9, 1954, to attacking the senator. Murrow used McCarthy's own words to deliver a damning picture of the senator and the threat to civil liberties that he posed.

Murrow's was not the first rallying cry against McCarthyism. Arthur Miller's 1953 play *The Crucible*, ostensibly about the Salem witch-hunt of the 1690s, had been a thinly veiled attack on it. But it was Murrow's broadcast that marked the start of McCarthy's fall from grace. Calls to CBS after the Murrow program were 15 to 1 in support of his view, and McCarthy's response, in his right-to-reply TV appearance, did not come over well. Irrational outbursts about the integrity of the armed forces further undermined his position, and by the end of the year McCarthy had been formally censured for conduct unbecoming a member of Congress. US abiding mistrust of communism, however, remains.

AT A GLANCE

With the USA and the Soviet Union bent on a superpower arms race, Senator Joseph McCarthy's one-man mission to seek out communist sympathizers in the nation's midst was over-zealous. His campaign caught many innocent people in the crossfire until Ed Murrow's intervention started to turn the tide.

Above: *Polio researcher Dr Jonas Salk giving a press conference in 1960.*

Right: US President Eisenhower commends Jonas Salk on the fifth anniversary of the doctor's development of a vaccine for polio, 1960.

Inset: A cryo-electron micrograph of the polio virus.

SUCCESSFUL POLIO VACCINE ANNOUNCED TO THE WORLD

UNIVERSITY OF PITTSBURGH, PA., USA

APRIL 12, 1955

Poliomyelitis is a virus that attacks the nervous system and usually occurs in children, causing deformation and paralysis. In the first half of the 20th century this disease affected hundreds of thousands worldwide and was considered a global epidemic. But all that changed in April 1955 when a cure was announced to the world.

The United States appeared to be a hotbed of the disease, which usually struck in the summer months. By the early 1950s, warmer weather was greeted each year with great anxiety, as yet more children and adults would be left dead or crippled by polio outbreaks. Even the late US President Franklin D. Roosevelt was believed to have been left paralyzed by the ailment.

The public reaction of sheer terror to this child-afflicting sickness meant that scientists around the world were racing to discover a cure, a vaccine that would reduce the increasing rate of death and paralysis and one that would herald a breakthrough in modern medicine.

The man who succeeded in this was US virologist Jonas Salk. After others had performed vaccination trials using live versions of polio which resulted in death and crippling, Salk believed protection could be achieved using deactivated forms of the virus. He predicted that by using the non-harmful version of polio, the human body would learn to reject the live form if and when it attacked. With large-scale outbreaks in 1952 and 1953 in the USA, the pressure was on for a resolution.

He had successfully created his vaccine in 1952, but the years of testing that followed prevented its immediate use. But it was in 1955 at his laboratory at the University of Pittsburgh that he was able to announce that the world's first effective vaccine for polio had been discovered.

It was the culmination of a three-year testing program, firstly on animals and later – and most crucially – on humans. Immediately, large-scale immunization programs for children were implemented across the country, and Salk was heralded as a savior.

Years later the virus had been effectively eradicated in the USA and most of the developed world, with cases drastically reduced to just a few thousand; a remarkable turnaround in just half a century.

AT A GLANCE

The epidemic disease known as polio was a danger to all, a fact underlined by news that even US President Franklin D. Roosevelt had suffered from it. The work of US scientist Jonas Salk in using a deactivated form of the virus to immunize children it saved generations from the scourge of this crippling disease.

Above: Civil rights pioneer Rosa Parks addresses a crowd celebrating the 25th anniversary of the signing of civil rights legislation.

Left: Rosa Parks in 1956, when the Supreme Court ruling banning segregation on Montgomery's public transport vehicles took effect.

ROSA PARKS REFUSES TO GIVE UP HER SEAT

MONTGOMERY, ALABAMA, USA

DECEMBER 1, 1955

'No one can understand the actions of Mrs Parks unless he realizes that eventually the cup of endurance runs over, and the human personality cries out, "I can take it no longer." ' So wrote Martin Luther King Jr in 1958. Three years earlier he had been a relatively unknown minister at the Dexter Avenue Baptist Church in Montgomery, Alabama – but then Rosa Parks said No.

When Parks, voluntary secretary of the Montgomery Chapter of the National Association for the Advancement of Colored People (NAACP), refused to vacate her bus seat for a white man after the 'white' section had been filled, she wasn't the first to do so in the segregated South. But that evening she had had enough. She became a focus for all the overflowing anger of the black community at the racist system of segregation which prevailed on buses and in other institutions across the southern states of the USA. "When that white driver stepped back towards [me]," she recalled, "I felt a determination cover my body like a quilt on a winter night."

The driver called the police, who arrested her for breaking the segregation laws. At her trial and conviction four days later, the black community began a boycott of the city buses which held solid for 381 days. In all weathers its 40,000 black commuters chose to share cars, take black-run taxis or walk (sometimes up to 20 miles), until their demands for black bus-drivers, common courtesy and bus seats on a first-come basis were met.

A new organization, the Montgomery Improvement Association, was formed to co-ordinate the boycott. Its president, a recent arrival in the neighborhood, was the young Martin Luther King Jr. His new position put him literally in the line of fire: churches were burned and his home bombed by segregationists during the boycott.

The NAACP won its legal challenge in the Supreme Court and segregation on buses was declared unconstitutional, and the boycott was called off the next day, December 20, 1956. But snipers opened fire on buses, and on King's home, which they also bombed again. King's leadership of the boycott had placed him at the head of the Civil Rights Movement, a powerful voice for its supporters and a dangerous target for its enemies.

Looking back, Rosa Parks commented, "People always say that I didn't give up my seat because I was tired, but that isn't true. No, the only tired I was, was tired of giving in."

AT A GLANCE

Rosa Parks's symbolic refusal to give up her seat for a white person in 1955 was used by civil rights campaigner Martin Luther King Jr as a focal point for protest. The struggle lasted a year, but was the first thread in the unraveling of segregation in the USA.

Above: Statesmen of six European countries sign the European Common Market Treaty in 1957.

Right: France's Robert Schuman (right), a strong advocate of European union, greeting West German Chancellor Konrad Adenauer.

TREATIES OF ROME

ITALY

MARCH 25, 1957

Winston Churchill, speaking in the neutral Swiss city of Zurich in 1946, called for 'a kind of United States of Europe' to be set up. The nations of Europe, exhausted by two world wars, were determined to put structures in place that would create a lasting peace.

The first step was the formation of West Germany, incorporating the larger part of the defeated nation into the economic life of the Western world. Then the Treaty of Paris in 1951, drawn up between Italy, France, Belgium, Luxembourg, West Germany and the Netherlands, formed the European Coal and Steel Community, a cross-border marketplace for those industries. It had been proposed a year earlier by the French foreign minister Robert Schuman as a means of making war 'not only unthinkable but materially impossible'.

This limited experiment in international cooperation was successful enough for the same six nations to extend the agreement. In 1957 they signed not one but two treaties in Rome. One set up Euratom, the European Atomic Energy Community, to develop mutual interests in nuclear power. The other, the one commentators mean when they talk about the Treaty of Rome, created the European Economic Community. The EEC was very much a trade-based organization, and became known as the Common Market.

Britain had declined to join the organization because they felt loyal to the many non-European countries that were members or former members of the British Empire or Commonwealth. Although Britain soon saw that it was missing out on EEC benefits, its applications for membership were repeatedly blocked by the French president, Charles de Gaulle. He wanted the EEC to become a third superpower, along with the USA and the USSR, and he objected to British ties with the USA. It was only after his death that Britain was able to negotiate entry to the EEC, which it achieved in 1973.

As the EEC expanded, so did its political aims. The first elections for the European Parliament took place in 1979. Border controls between many of its members were ended by the Shengen Agreement in 1985, and the community dropped the word 'economic' in 1986, becoming the European Union (EU). The fall of communism in 1990 saw the community's rapid expansion eastwards. Then in 2002 the common currency of the Euro was first introduced; by 2010, 16 out of 27 EU member states were using it.

Most of the participating countries consider they have reaped an economic benefit so far as commerce is concerned. While debate about the extent of European political union remains far from peaceful, military war between members of the EU is, as Schuman envisaged, unimaginable.

AT A GLANCE

In the aftermath of the Second World War, world leaders were keen to form alliances that would minimise the chance of another conflict and at the same time encourage economic regeneration through trade. Britain's ties with the Commonwealth left the British outside the European Economic Community, which it eventually joined in 1973. By 2010 its original membership had swelled to 27 countries thanks in part to the admission of former communist states.

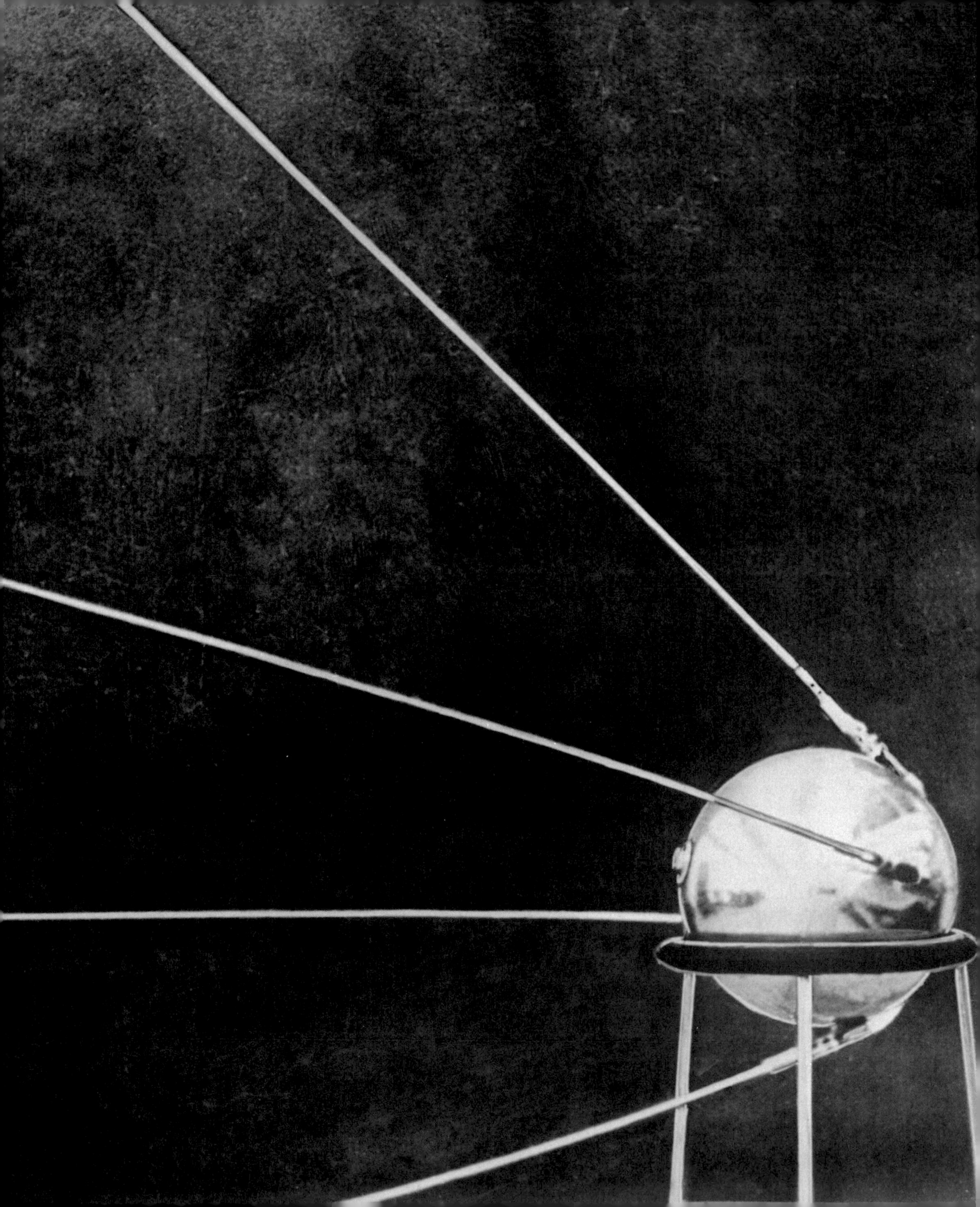

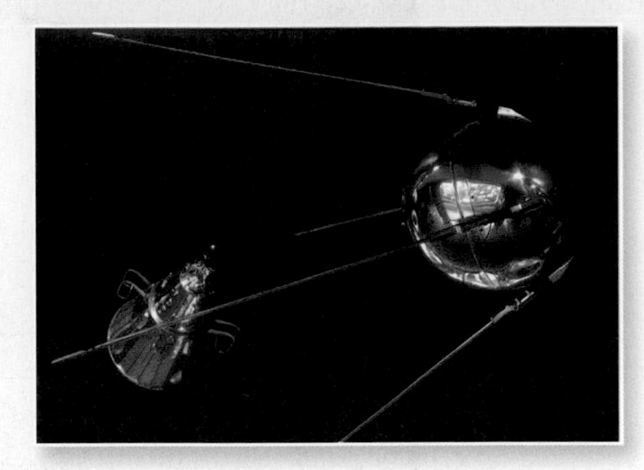

Above: A back-up version of Sputnik 1 (right) and a replica of Sputnik 2 in a Moscow museum.

Left: Sputnik 1 resting on a metal stand before it was sent into space. The four projecting rods are the satellite's antennae.

Below: This diagram compares the relative orbits of Sputnik 3 and the three orbiting US satellites, Explorer I, Vanguard I, and Explorer III.

THE LAUNCH OF SPUTNIK 1

TYURATAM, KAZAKHSTAN
OCTOBER 4, 1957

The launch of the satellite Sputnik 1 is generally celebrated as the start of the space race between the USA and the Soviet Union. Whatever the motivation, the rush to reach milestones in extraterrestrial exploration drove the two governments to inspiring voyages of discovery in science and space unimagined 30 years before. Although huge amounts of government money have been spent on the projects, the benefit to humanity from technologies first developed for the exploration of space is already incalculable, and although future exploration is subject to political whim, its potential is as vast as the universe.

The first rival steps in the Space Race were arguably taken not in 1957 but in the summer of 1955, within ten days of each other. On July 29 that year, the USA announced that one of its key scientific events planned for the International Geophysical Year, 1957–58, would be the launch of an artificial satellite; and on August 9, the Soviet Union gave an identical go-ahead for the Sputnik program.

In the USA, the job of development was given to the US Naval Research Laboratory. But while they were working on a test vehicle for the first stage of their Vanguard launch rocket, news reached them of the successful launch by the USSR of Sputnik 1 on October 4, 1957. The blow to US pride echoed round the globe. To add insult to injury, Russia encouraged the world's radio operators to record the satellite's beep-beep signal as it passed 150 miles overhead every 96 minutes.

Sputnik 2 soon followed, carrying Laika the dog into space on November 3. The catastrophic failure of two US Vanguard launches over the next four months only deepened US gloom, and the US navy was embarrassed even more when the US army's rival Explorer 1 (hastily revived after the triumph of Sputnik 1) became the USA's first artificial satellite, on February 1, 1958. The eventual success of Vanguard 1, on March 17 that year, was swiftly overshadowed by the launch of Sputnik 3 two months later.

Vanguard 1 was the first solar-powered satellite, and the US navy may take comfort in the fact that it has outlived all its predecessors; it transmitted for seven years, and in 2010 it is still up there while its predecessors have dropped out of orbit and burnt up on re-entry. Sputnik 1's conventional batteries powered its information-laden beeps for a mere three weeks, and it fell back to Earth, mission accomplished, on January 4, 1958.

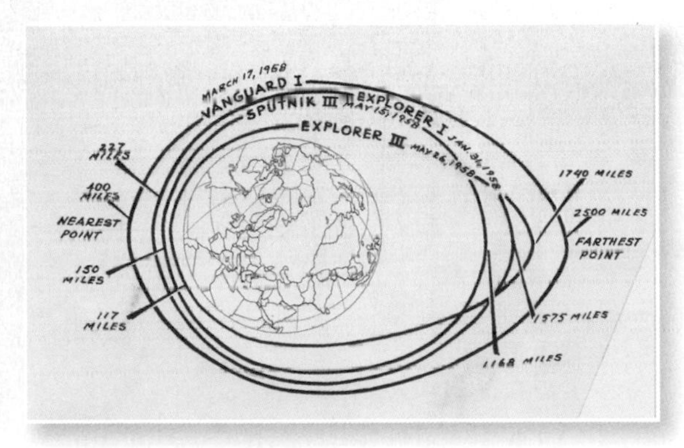

AT A GLANCE

The quest for national prestige led the USA and the Soviet Union, the world's nuclear superpowers, to push the boundaries and attempt to put a satellite into earth orbit. Sputnik 1 won the first round of the Space Race for the USSR, and the Russians also put the first man into space, three and a half years later.

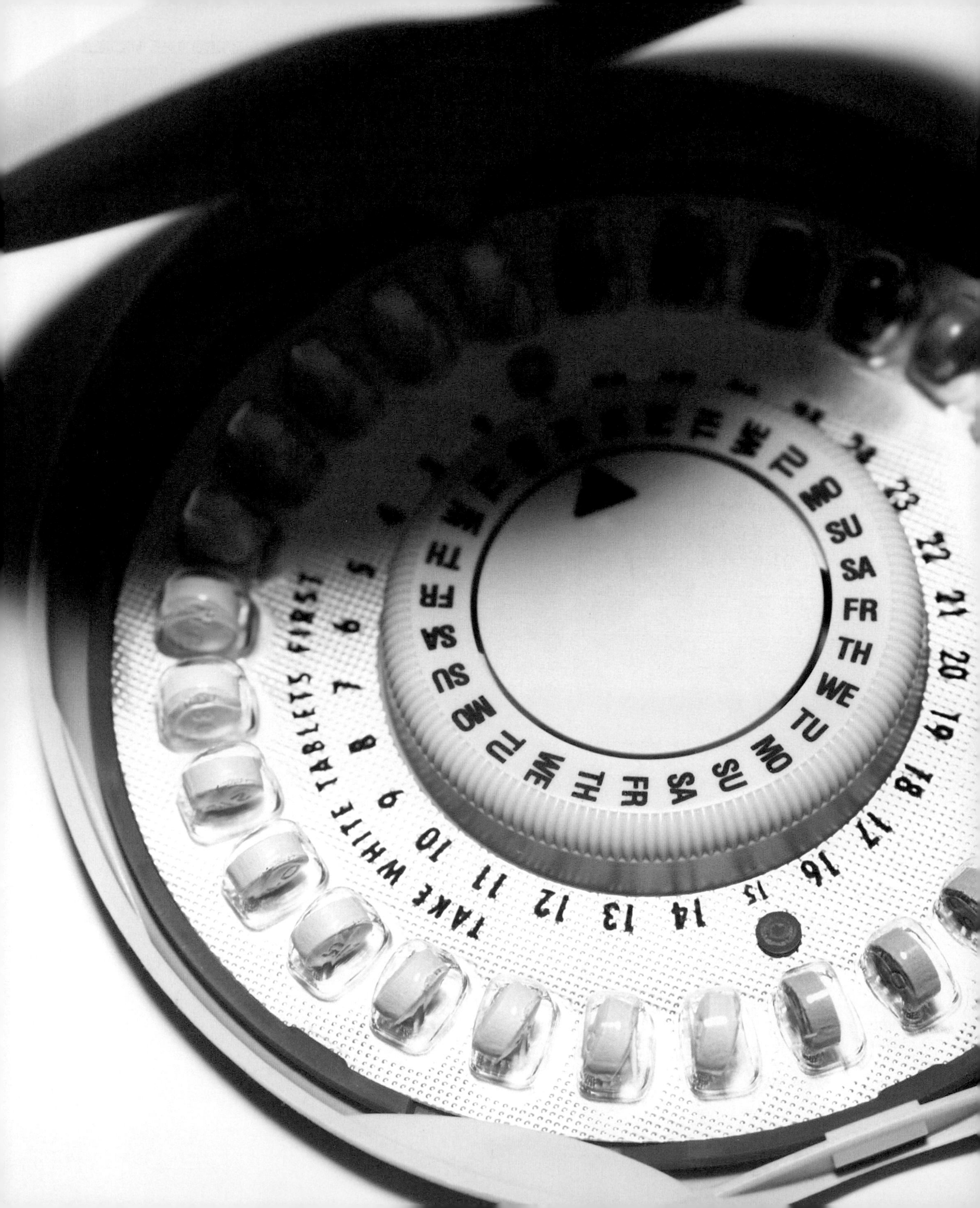
TAKE WHITE TABLETS FIRST
5 6 7 8 9 10 11 12 13 14 15 16 17 18 19 20 21 22 23 24
TH FR SA SU MO TU WE TH FR SA SU MO TU WE TH FR SA SU MO TU WE

ORAL CONTRACEPTIVE PILL APPROVED

USA
MAY 9, 1960

After being tested in Puerto Rico and Haiti in 1956, the oral contraceptive pill was approved by the US Food and Drug Administration on May 9, 1960. It went on sale in the USA in the spring of 1961 under the brand names Enovid and Norlutin, the price for a four-week supply being $10.

The Pill, as it universally became known, has been described as the most significant medical advance of the 20th century. It was developed by American biologist Dr Gregory Pincus, who had been approached in 1953 by family planning pioneers Margaret Sanger and Katherine McCormick. He was able to build on the research of Frank Colton, a chemist at the Searle Company, and in 1957 the Pill was released as a treatment for gynecological disorders.

The first version contained the hormones estrogen and progestin, which were synthetically produced to mimic the body's natural hormones and suppress ovulation. In the early years, the Pill contained around 50 mcg of estrogen, and this has since been reduced to around 30 mcg due to health concerns. Progestin levels have been reduced to a tenth of their original level.

The Pill allowed women greater sexual freedom. Within five years, 40 per cent of married US women under age 30 who used contraception were using the Pill. But its influence grew still further in the early 1970s when the age of majority was reduced to 18 years. Young, single women could now 'go on the Pill', and within a couple of years, 73 per cent of all single women age 18 and 19 using contraception were using the Pill.

The Puerto Rican study had been monitored for adverse side effects; one in five women reported nausea and/or weight gain. Preliminary findings showed a reduction in breast and uterine cancer, but health worries persisted: after congressional hearings on the Pill's safety, the US Food and Drug Administration was prompted in 1970 to order drug manufacturers to provide information about possible risks and side effects with each prescription package; these warnings were a first for any prescription drug.

In the USA, the number of users fell in the early 1980s from around 10 million women to around 8.4 million because of the concerns. Research suggested possible links between use of the Pill and breast cancer, strokes, heart attack and blood clots. Some of the concerns were linked to the hormone levels in the pill; these have now been lowered again.

Above: Dr Gregory Pincus, the man regarded as the inventor of the contraceptive pill.

Left: A pack of birth control pills, as used by millions of women around the world.

AT A GLANCE

The development of an oral contraceptive pill, preventing pregnancy by suppressing ovulation, has been described as the most significant medical advance of the 20th century. It gave women the ability to control their fertility and inevitably opened the doors to increased sexual activity, for better or worse. The Swinging Sixties was on the horizon ...

Above: *How the US nation viewed the first televised presidential debate between Vice President Richard Nixon and Senator John F. Kennedy in 1960.*

Right: *Presidential nominees Kennedy and Nixon meet, prior to their first debate.*

Below: *A large crowd gathered to greet Kennedy as he arrived in Chicago for his televised debate.*

FIRST TELEVISED PRESIDENTIAL DEBATE

CHICAGO, USA
SEPTEMBER 26, 1960

Republican Vice President Richard Nixon and his Democratic opponent, Senator John F. Kennedy, took part in the first ever televised US Presidential debate in 1960. It took place in the Chicago television studio of WBBM-TV and was carried by all major US television and radio stations.

Questions were posed by representatives of the TV channels NBC, CBS, ABC and Mutual, with Howard K. Smith of CBS acting as moderator. The one-hour show saw both candidates score points, Nixon claiming that Kennedy's proposed spending program would cost the taxpayers billions of dollars while Kennedy accused the vice president of 'paying only lip service' to the concept of increasing the minimum wage to a dollar an hour. Kennedy also attacked Nixon's plans for building more schools and health care for the aged, as being inferior to his own.

The show attracted over 66 million viewers out of a population of 179 million, making it one of the most-watched broadcasts in US television history. Yet most viewers polled after watching the show said their voting intentions had not been changed. But when the election on November 8 was won by Kennedy by a narrow margin, the televised debate was thought to have made the difference in what was an extremely close election.

Kennedy, 43 years old to Nixon's 47, was considered more televisual. He had recently returned from vacation and was tanned and relaxed, his navy suit standing out better than Nixon's grey, which blended into the background. Nixon himself had a somewhat haggard appearance due not only to his refusal to wear television make-up but also to fatigue; he had recently been hospitalized for a knee operation and, according to one commentator, appeared 'unshaven, tired and sweaty' under the lights.

It was not until 1976 that a second series of televised presidential debates was held during the election campaign, this time between Jimmy Carter and Gerald Ford. Since then, these televised debates have been a regular feature in the hustings, as have vice-presidential debates. The UK adopted the format for the first time in 2010, when leaders of the Labour, Liberal Democrat and Conservative parties all took part in a three-way debate.

AT A GLANCE

The first ever televised US Presidential debate took place in 1960 between Richard Nixon and John F. Kennedy. While its effect on the result could not be measured, from this moment on the new medium of television played an ever-growing part in presidential elections. Candidate-centered television campaigns were launched, and it became important for politicians to be well versed in the arts of communicating via the camera.

MRBM FIELD LAUNCH SITE
SAN CRISTOBAL NO 1
14 OCTOBER 1962
ERECTOR/LAUNCHER EQUIPMENT
EQUIPMENT
TENT AREAS
ERECTOR/LAUNCHER EQUIPMENT
8 MISSILE TRAILERS
CONSTRUCTION

AT A GLANCE

One and a half decades of superpower posturing came to a head in 1962 when the USA and the Soviet Union focused on the Caribbean island of Cuba, where Soviet missile sites had been established, and stared each other down; the first one to blink might possibly ignite a worldwide nuclear conflict. However, the standoff was resolved, the missiles were removed and an uneasy détente was established.

KHRUSHCHEV AGREES TO REMOVE MISSILES

CUBA
OCTOBER 28, 1962

In 1961 the USA made an effort, with an invasion of US-trained Cuban exiles, to overthrow Cuba's communist regime, but failed embarrassingly. The exiles, landing at the Bay of Pigs on the island, were defeated within three days by the USSR-backed Cuban army.

It was a humiliation which former US President Eisenhower had predicted would 'embolden the Soviets to do something that they would otherwise not do' – and 18 months later the Russians began to install nuclear missiles on the strategically important island of Cuba. It was a response to continuing US harassment of the island on land and by sea, as well as the installation of US missiles in Turkey, in easy striking range of Moscow.

US U-2 reconnaissance planes first spotted the new missile sites in Cuba on October 15, 1962, and a week later President Kennedy announced a naval blockade of the island to prevent the arrival of further warheads. He declared that any attack launched from Cuba on any target would be considered an attack on the USA, and liable to a counter-attack on the USSR.

For two weeks the world held its breath as troops massed in Florida, the nearest mainland point to Cuba. The US military commanders, as hawkish as ever, had argued for a pre-emptive invasion of Cuba, and Kennedy assured them that if Cuba shot down any US spyplanes he would authorize an attack on the missile sites. It seemed a very real possibility that the USA and the USSR would soon be at nuclear war with each other. According to the media, this had the overwhelming support of Americans, but it resulted in anti-war demonstrations around the world.

In the end, the Soviet ships turned back without trying to breach the US blockade. The Soviet leader, Nikita Khrushchev, offered to remove the missiles in return for a promise that the USA would not invade Cuba. But while Kennedy was discussing this offer with his staff, news arrived of the shooting down of a US spy plane over Cuba, triggering fresh demands on Kennedy for a military assault. He, however, correctly deduced that it was an isolated action by a rogue Soviet officer, and instead of ordering a retaliation accepted Khrushchev's terms.

The Cuban missile crisis led directly to the establishment of a hotline between the White House and the Kremlin, and to the quiet removal three months later of US missiles in Turkey. It was a landmark of common sense in Cold War diplomacy. Two superpowers had stepped back from the brink, and the world breathed again.

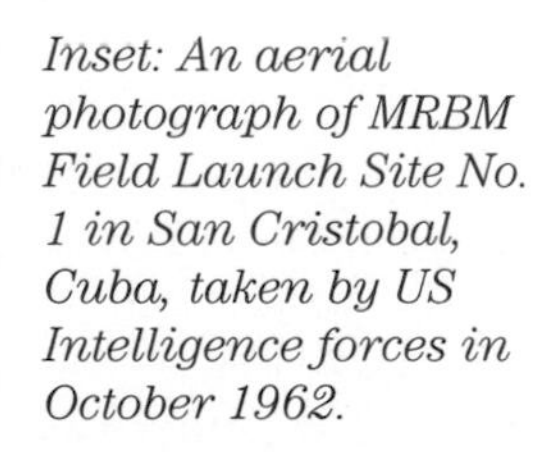

Inset: An aerial photograph of MRBM Field Launch Site No. 1 in San Cristobal, Cuba, taken by US Intelligence forces in October 1962.

Left: The Soviet freighter Anosov *leaves Cuba with eight ballistic missiles on board as the crisis eases.*

Above: Leaders of the March on Washington link arms as they move along Constitution Avenue. Martin Luther King is seventh from right.

Right: Thousands of people gather at the Lincoln Memorial and around its reflecting pool to hear featured speakers at the conclusion of the March on Washington.

Below: Martin Luther King Jr gives his famous 'I Have a Dream' speech in front of the Lincoln Memorial.

MARCH ON WASHINGTON, DC

USA

AUGUST 28, 1963

In 1963, US President John F. Kennedy's government was working towards passing a civil rights bill meant to bring the USA into the modern world by creating racial equality in society, employment and education. But even though it was eight years after Rosa Parks had said No, entrenched prejudices still held sway in certain states, especially in the Deep South.

A civil rights march on the nation's capital, Washington, DC, planned for August 28, 1963, was intended to show support for the proposed bill and raise awareness of the inequalities still suffered by millions of black people in the USA at the time.

The figurehead was clergyman Dr Martin Luther King Jr, but in reality the march was a collective effort made by many different factions of the civil rights movement. It was chiefly organized by Asa Philip Randolph, chairman of civil rights faction The Brotherhood of Sleeping Car Porters. But not all civil rights campaigners were on board, most notably Malcolm X, head of religious faction The Nation of Islam, who did not participate in the march and strongly criticized it, saying that white participation in it was counterproductive.

The event went ahead regardless, with over 250,000 people converging on Washington, DC, in the largest public protest in the USA's history. The march ended at the Lincoln Memorial, where there were speeches from leaders and music from artists sympathetic to the cause, including folk singers Bob Dylan and Joan Baez.

The highlight of the event was an emotive and inspiring sermon-style speech by Martin Luther King that was picked up by US television and the international media. The most quoted line was: 'I have a dream that one day this nation will rise up and live out the true meaning of its creed. We hold these truths to be self-evident, that all men are created equal'.

The Kennedy civil rights bill was passed in 1964, outlawing segregation and allowing all men and women in the USA to vote. And while racism might not have been eradicated, the bill paved the way for change, ultimately resulting in the election of America's first black president, Barack Obama, in 2009.

The 1963 March on Washington was a pivotal moment in not just US but world history. Martin Luther King, like President Kennedy, died a violent death and never saw the full fruits of his struggle, but the change in American society that he helped create was undeniable.

AT A GLANCE

Martin Luther King's 'I have a dream' speech, delivered from the steps of the Lincoln Memorial in the US capital in 1963, inspired a generation and encapsulated the cause of racial equality. It has been voted top American speech of the 20th century.

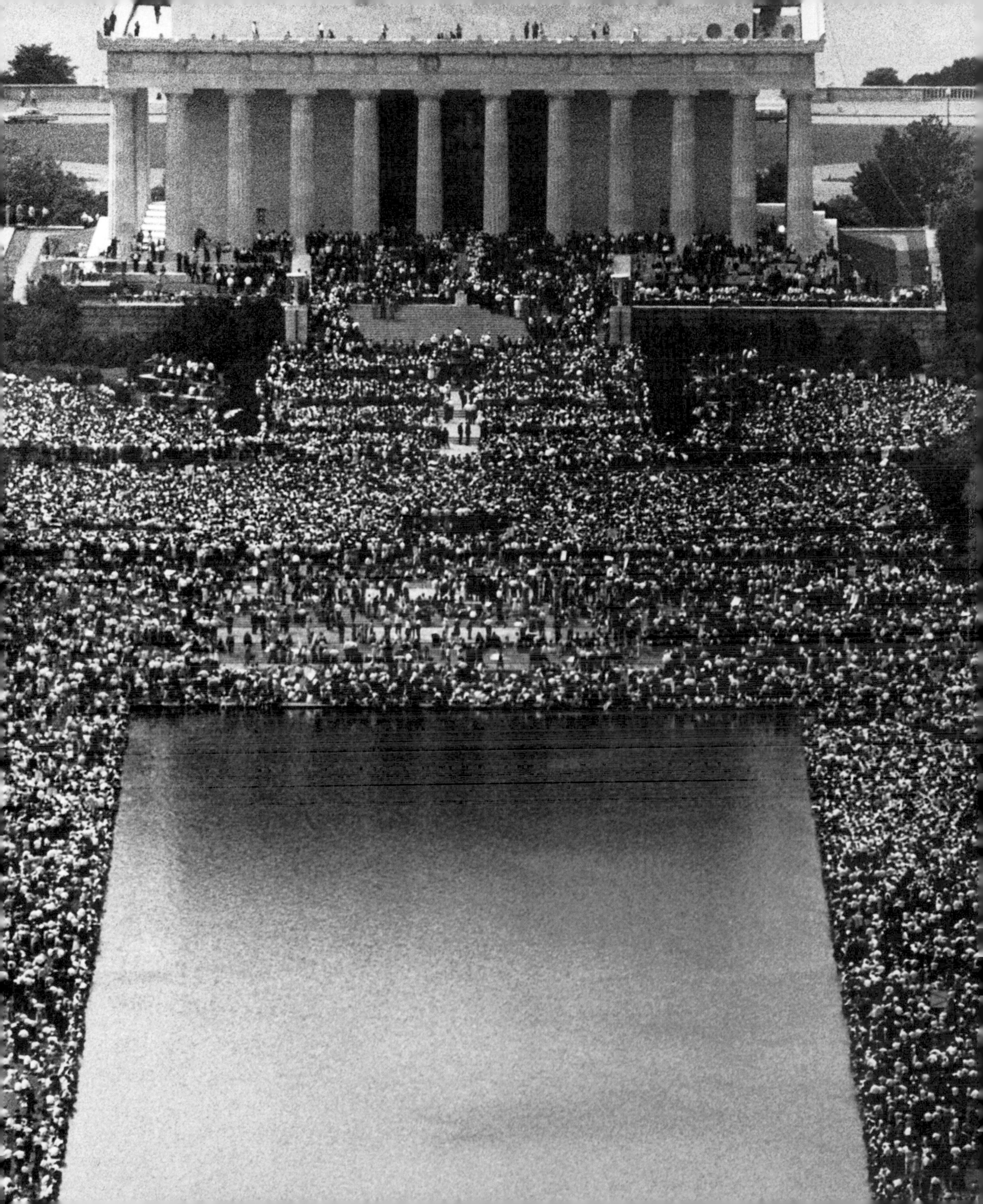

Above: Jacqueline Kennedy watches as her husband's body is placed in an ambulance at Andrews Air Force Base.

Left: President Kennedy, First Lady Jacqueline Kennedy, and Texas Governor John Connally ride in the motorcade in Dallas, moments before the President and the Governor were shot.

ASSASSINATION OF PRESIDENT KENNEDY

DALLAS, TEXAS, USA
NOVEMBER 22, 1963

When President John F. Kennedy was assassinated in Dealey Plaza in downtown Dallas in 1963, the bullets ricocheted around the world. It caused the death of a postwar optimism and innocence which had flourished in the economic prosperity of the 1950s. That bullet, in taking the life of the USA's virile and youthful leader, also affected millions who admired him. In the days that followed, most of the world felt stunned.

People simply could not believe that anyone would want to kill such a popular figure, and that disbelief has expressed itself ever since in the many conspiracy theories – often conflicting with one another – that have arisen almost from the moment JFK was hit. One gunman or two – the Mafia – the FBI – the CIA – pro-Castro Cubans, anti-Castro Cubans – even Vice President Lyndon B. Johnson … all these and more have been the focus for elaborately conceived 'solutions' to the murder.

The official version of events is that a single gunman, Lee Harvey Oswald, fired on the presidential motorcade from his place of work, the Texas School Book Depository, overlooking the plaza. Oswald was a mentally unstable ex-Marine who had defected to the Soviet Union and then returned to the USA where, seven months before Dallas, he had tried to assassinate a retired US major-general. Oswald denied involvement in Kennedy's assassination, and the truth may never be known: he was shot dead two days later by Jack Ruby, a Dallas nightclub owner who, it is said, took it upon himself to avenge the USA's loss.

At least five separate investigations into the shooting of President Kennedy have taken place since then. The Warren Commission was the first, set up by newly sworn-in President Johnson a week after the event. It found that Oswald had acted alone in committing the crime – but a 1979 enquiry by the House Select Committee on Assassinations lent weight to the possibility that a second gunman was involved, who fired (and missed) from a grassy knoll on the other side of the car.

To this day every witness statement, every audio or video recording, and every artifact of evidence from the scene is examined and re-examined in the hope of new insight into the who and why of JFK's assassination. In 1981 one author even had Oswald's body exhumed.

AT A GLANCE

The assassin of the 35th president of the USA has still not been definitively identified, despite the fact that the event was captured on film. What is certain is that the charismatic 46-year-old who had defeated Richard Nixon in the 1960 US presidential election still had much he wanted to achieve.

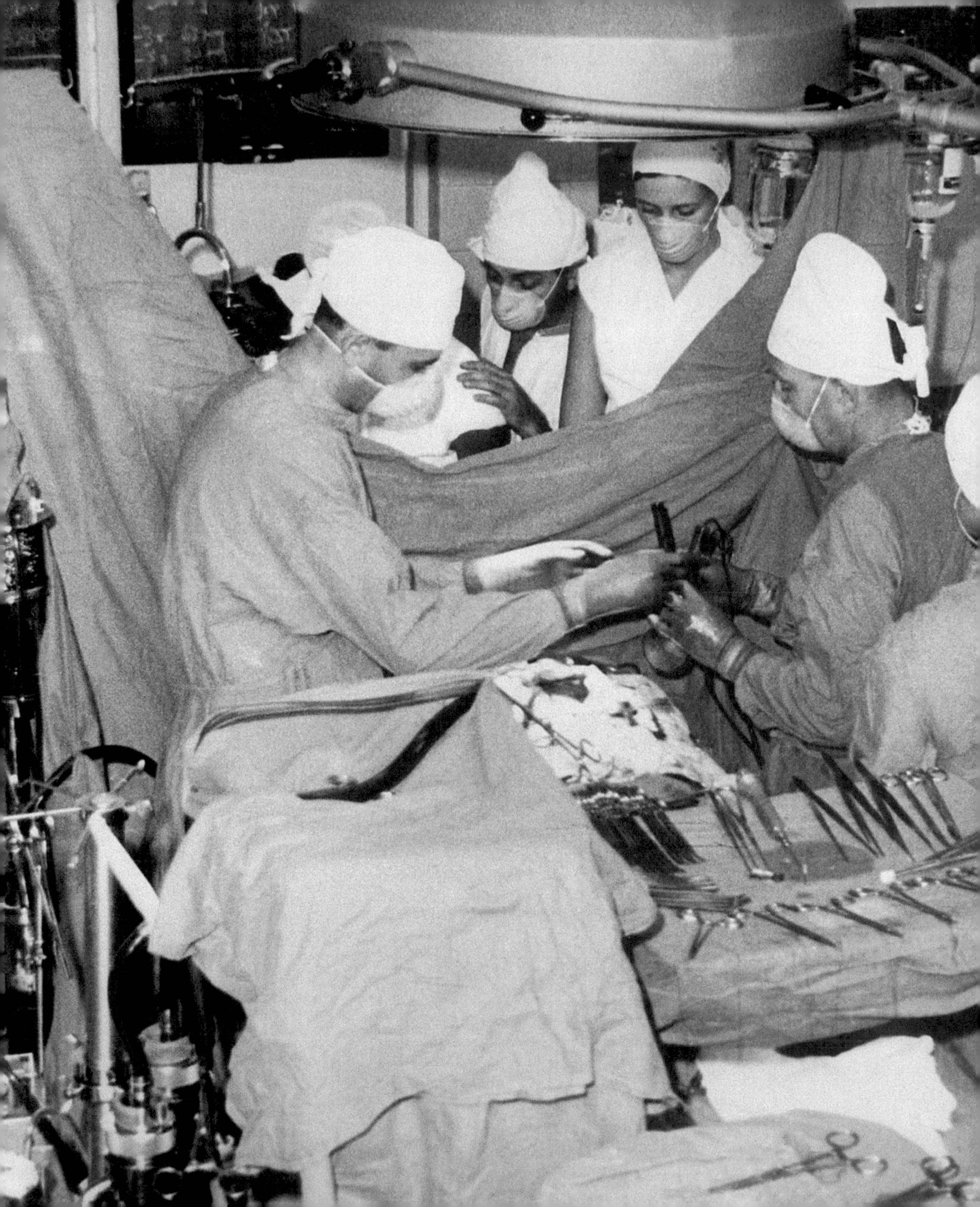

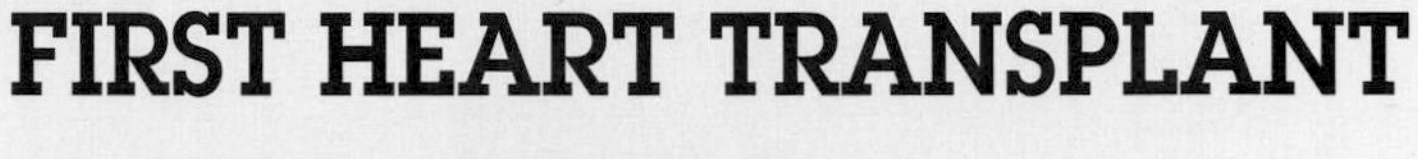

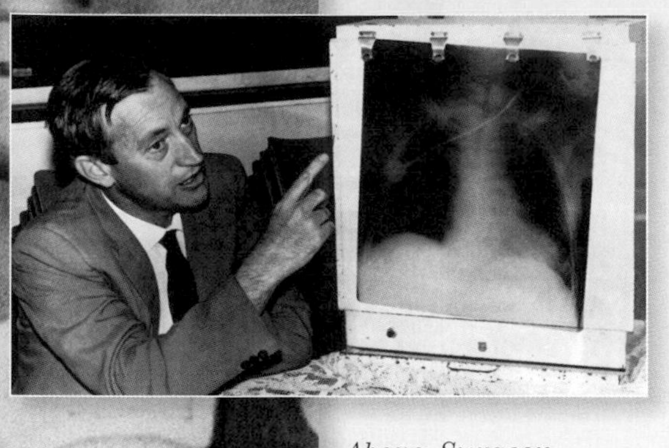

FIRST HEART TRANSPLANT

CAPE TOWN, SOUTH AFRICA
DECEMBER 3, 1967

In 1967 an operation was carried out in Cape Town, South Africa, that revolutionized surgery as we knew it, and started the ball rolling on a procedure that would save millions of lives. On December 3, Christiaan Barnard completed the world's first full heart transplant.

Above: Surgeon Christiaan Barnard shows an X-ray image of Louis Washkansky's chest taken during the historic first heart transplant.

Left: Members of Christiaan Barnard's surgical team perform open-heart surgery in the theater where the Washkansky operation was carried out.

Below: Louis Washkansky, the middle-aged grocer who accepted the heart of Denise Darvall.

Barnard was a surgeon from Beaufort West, South Africa, who had travelled to the USA as a 34-year-old postgraduate in 1956, specializing in cardiac surgery. He returned to South Africa two years later, to the Groote Schuur Hospital teaching facility where he began his career with a residency, assembling its first cardiac team.

He prepared for the milestone procedure by performing South Africa's first kidney transplant, in October 1967. He was already seen as one of the country's top surgeons, and with several completed heart transplants on animals the next step was clear.

The patient was chosen; Louis Washkansky had incurable heart disease and, at 54, was still relatively young. With the end in sight, he had no hesitation in agreeing to the operation. His donor had to come through tragic circumstance, in the form of Denise Darvall, a young woman killed in a road accident.

Barnard's 30-strong team, including his brother Marius, took five hours to complete the transplant from Darvall to Washkansky, but at its conclusion the heart was beating with no mechanical assistance. Tragedy struck just 18 days later, however, as Washkansky died from severe pneumonia; his fragile immune system could not resist the infection so soon after the procedure.

Despite this, the transplant was considered a huge success, as Washkansky's new heart continued to beat unaided right up until his death. Further attempts were longer-lasting, with one patient, Dirk van Zyl, living on for 23 years after his 1971 operation, to the age of 68.

Since the first surgery, thousands of people have undergone successful heart transplants, though a lack of donors has kept the number from rising faster. British surgeon Sir Terrence English performed the world's first heart and lung transplant in 1984.

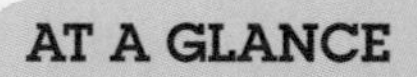

AT A GLANCE

The actions of Christiaan Barnard and his team of surgeons in South Africa in 1967 set a new benchmark in surgical procedures. In transplanting a working heart from one human being to another it furthered our ability to prolong life, and it was a truly world-changing achievement.

Above: Astronaut Neil Armstrong leaves a footprint on the surface of the Moon at Tranquility Base.

Right: Buzz Aldrin stands beside an American flag at Tranquility Base on the surface of the moon during the Apollo 11 *mission.*

Overleaf: Buzz Aldrin heads back to the Lunar Module Eagle *having deployed an array of scientific testing equipment.*

MAN LANDS ON THE MOON

JULY 20, 1969

It was an event so unbelievable and significant that some claim it did not even occur, and conspiracy theories persist to this day. But when the pictures of a man walking on the moon was shown live in 1969, the world watched in awe.

The United States and the Soviet Union had been involved in what had been dubbed the Space Race since the Soviet's launch of its Sputnik 1 *satellite* in 1957. Both nations wanted to be considered the planet's dominant force, on land and on sea, in the air and in space; the high point of that dominance would be landing the first human on the moon. With millions of dollars ploughed into the North American Space Administration (NASA), it was the USA that won the race, with the Apollo 11 mission launching on July 16, 1969.

Its crew was headed by former navy aviator Neil Armstrong, accompanied by fellow astronauts Michael Collins and Edwin 'Buzz' Aldrin. Their Saturn V rocket blasted off from the Kennedy Space Center in Florida just after 9.30 a.m., aiming to make history. Four days later, the lunar module *Eagle*, manned by Armstrong and Aldrin, detached from the Columbia command module that still contained Collins, and began its descent to the moon's surface. Their destination was a lunar plain known as the Sea of Tranquility. On reaching the surface, Armstrong reported, "Houston, Tranquility Base here. The *Eagle* has landed."

Six and a half hours after landing on the surface, Neil Armstrong became the first man to set foot on the moon. With 600 million eyes watching on Earth, he uttered the immortal words, "That's one small step for man, one giant leap for mankind."

Aldrin soon joined him and the pair spent time photographing the surface and the lunar module and taking soil samples for analysis before planting a US flag. They talked over a radio phone with President Richard Nixon, which he described as 'the most historic phone call ever made from the White House'.

The crew of Apollo 11 splashed back down on Earth on July 24, in the middle of the Pacific Ocean. Picked up by a US Navy vessel, they returned to land and spent three weeks in quarantine. They emerged to mass adulation and fame, the only three humans in history to have set foot on another body in space.

The Apollo program saw six more lunar landings completed in the next three years, before NASA's budget decreased and attention turned to other experiments. But it is the moment when a man took his first steps on the moon that linger in the memory.

AT A GLANCE

One man's first steps on the moon ended the sixties on an optimistic note, allowing the USA to forget Vietnam and the Kennedy assassination, and celebrate the achievement of winning the 'Space Race'. Neil Armstrong and his crew made history, even if subsequent decades have seen the focus of exploration switched elsewhere.

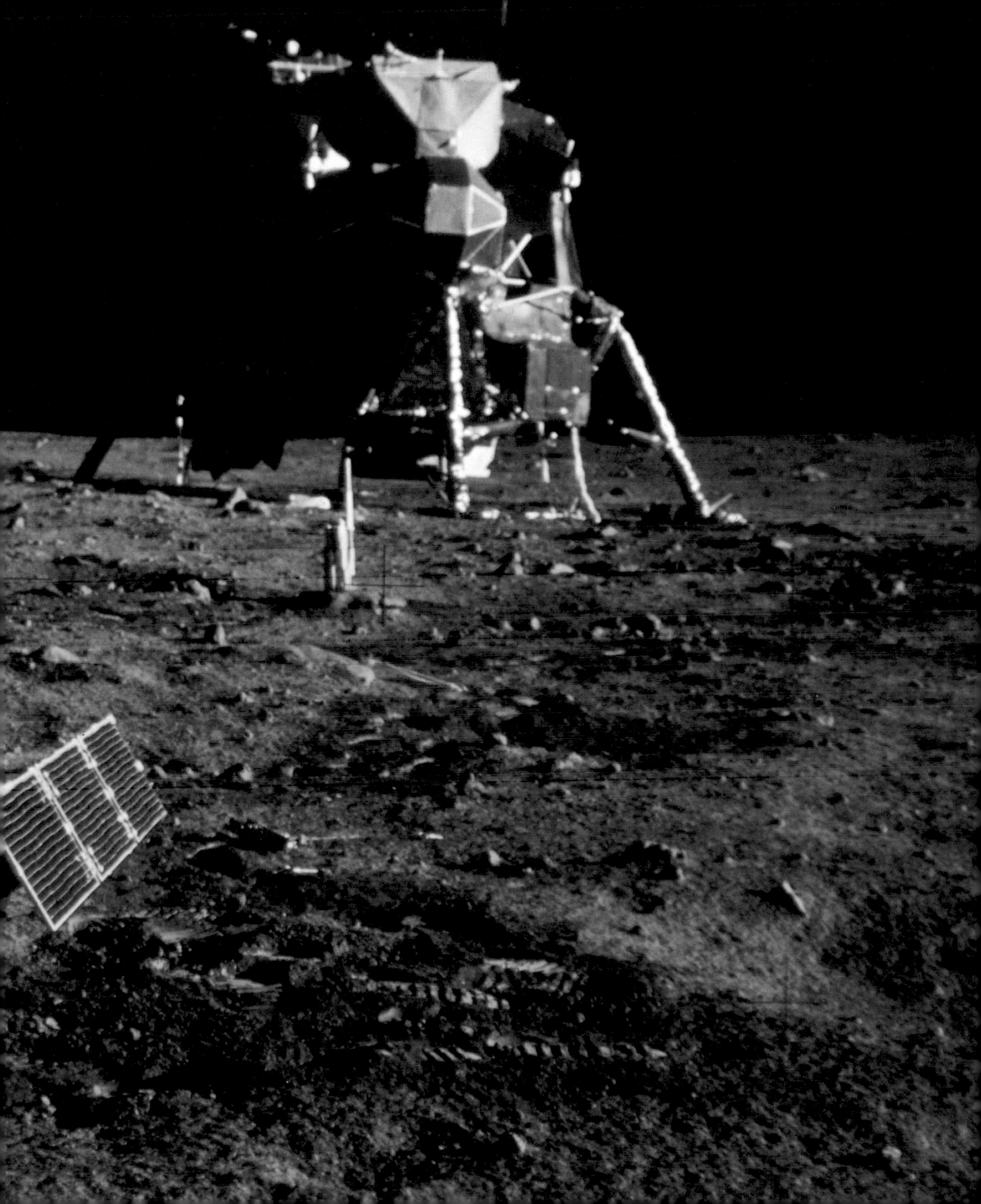

Above: President Nixon meets with children wearing Mao Tse-tung buttons during his visit to China.

Left: President of the United States of America Richard Nixon and Premier of the People's Republic of China, Zhou Enlai, applaud a sports contest in China, during Nixon's historic 1972 visit to the country.

PRESIDENT NIXON VISITS CHINA

CHINA

FEBRUARY 21, 1972

It was an unexpected olive branch that would become a historic event. After two decades of acrimonious relations between the two countries, US President Richard Nixon took the surprise step of visiting the People's Republic of China, in a move that would begin the healing process between the two countries.

At his inauguration in 1968, Nixon proclaimed, "The greatest honor history can bestow is the title of peacemaker." But few then would have predicted his actions a few years later; on his election, Nixon, along with the whole of America, had been a determined opponent of communism, and the country was at odds with the Soviet Union because of it. With China a communist nation, there looked to be no amicable future between the two, either.

There were however a few factors behind Nixon's visit; the US general election was just months away, and his critics would argue that improving the long-running poor relations with China would be beneficial to his re-election campaign.

Also, the meeting between US and Chinese table tennis athletes Glenn Cowan and Zhuang Zedong, which had been covered in the press and adopted by the Chinese as an official diplomatic move by the USA, provided evidence of a thaw in relations between the two countries.

After the foundations had been laid by Nixon's national security advisor, Henry Kissinger, in a secret visit the previous year, the President landed on Chinese soil on February 21, 1972. The week-long visit provided a visual treat for the American media, with some of the first images of China being broadcast in nearly two decades. Behind the PR masterpiece, however, was the intention of creating a new alliance, punctuated by an immediate meeting with China's leader, Chairman Mao.

The conclusion of the visit saw the announcement and signing of the Shanghai Communiqué, which outlined the intention of the USA and China to create a stronger relationship, though the USA's ambiguous stance on the ownership of Taiwan would prevent a complete normalization of relations. Seven years later, full diplomatic relations were achieved between the two countries; this was announced in the Joint Communiqué on the Establishment of Diplomatic Relations of 1979.

The initial surprise of Nixon's visit to China was eclipsed by the seven-day media circus that followed, and the positive diplomatic outcome. Nixon described his visit as 'the week that changed the world.'

AT A GLANCE

President Nixon's unexpected overtures to China in the early seventies broke two decades of silence between the USA and China. It was an act which, together with his similar attempts at a rapprochement with the Soviet Union, earned the president a second term in the White House.

Above: *The last planeload of US troops out of Vietnam arrives home, March 1973.*

Left: *Alan L. Brunstrom, a recently released prisoner of war, greets his family on his arrival at Travis Air Force Base, California, 1973.*

Below: *American soldiers relax with their baggage as they await their flight home, March 1973.*

US TROOPS LEAVE VIETNAM

VIETNAM
MARCH 29, 1973

After over 13 years, and in spite of determined opposition from large sections of the USA, in 1973 President Nixon finally declared his country's withdrawal from the conflict in Vietnam.

America's disillusionment with the war and how it was handled reached a climax in the aftermath of the Tet Offensive of 1968; the force of the communist attack had brought the realization that the conflict was far from over, as had been suggested earlier, and a beleaguered President Johnson did not run for re-election.

The escalation of the USA's involvement had fatally damaged Johnson's presidency, and it looked to continue with Nixon at the helm; the bombing of Cambodia in March 1969 and the number of US fatalities rising above 33,000 both had a strong negative effect on public opinion.

Despite the removal of 25,000 troops in June 1969, the exposing of the My Lai massacre five months later in which more than 500 innocent Vietnamese were killed by rampaging American troops, and then the Kent State Shootings of May 1970 in which four students were shot dead by the National Guard, only served to increase protestors' resolve. The US presence in South Vietnam continued to decrease steadily; at the turn of 1972 just over 130,000 troops remained.

The end of the war – as far as America was concerned – was in sight as that year came to a close. The Paris Peace Accords signed by North Vietnam and the USA on January 27, 1973, declared a ceasefire throughout southeast Asia (Vietnam, Cambodia and Laos); the USA would withdraw its remaining troops, and American prisoners of war would be returned. The agreement recognized the South Vietnamese government remaining in power under President Thieu, but also permitted North Vietnamese troops to remain in the South.

On March 29, 1973, two months after the peace agreement, Hanoi freed the remaining American prisoners of war and the last US troops left South Vietnam, but 7,000 employees of the US Department of Defense remained in South Vietnam to aid the ongoing battle. North Vietnam eventually took South Vietnam's capital Saigon in April 1975.

It was a blow for the US's policy of containment, but the conflict had raged for so long that priorities had shifted. Nixon had turned his attention to détente with the Soviet Union and China, a policy that had succeeded in getting him re-elected for a second term. He also achieved popular support for ending the longest war in the country's history.

AT A GLANCE

The Vietnam War had always been controversial, and President Nixon's decision to withdraw in 1973 finally recognized the fact that this particular part of the USA's global battle against communism could not be won. The majority of Americans agreed with him, some 50,000 US troops and nearly two million Vietnamese having lost their lives.

Above: Sheikh Ahmed Zaki Yamani, Saudi Arabia's Oil Minister, attends talks on the oil crisis, 1973.

Right: The sign speaks for itself – US motorists run on empty during the 1973 oil crisis.

OIL CRISIS

KUWAIT

OCTOBER 1973

The 1973 oil crisis began in October of that year when members of Organization of Arab Petroleum Exporting Countries (OAPEC), based in Kuwait, instigated an oil embargo against the USA and its allies in response to US support for Israel in the Yom Kippur war. The catalyst had been the request by President Nixon to Congress to put $2.2 billion towards emergency aid to Israel.

President Nixon asked US citizens to cut back on oil consumption to reduce the effects of the embargo: he asked gas stations to close voluntarily on Sundays, ordered a cutback on home heating oil deliveries and a 15 per cent cut in gas consumption, and reduced speed limits to 50 mph. He believed the combination of measures would reduce the shortfall in supply from 17 per cent to 7 per cent. In Britain, meanwhile, a three-day working week was adopted.

By February 1974, over half the gas stations in New York area had closed for lack of supplies, while lines up to six miles long were observed at stations that were open. The price of crude oil, which in October 1973 had risen by 70 per cent to $5.11 a barrel, rose to over $10 per barrel, Libya posting the record of $18.77.

The Nixon administration also began negotiations with Israel to pull back from the Sinai and the Golan Heights, territories it had claimed. The promise of a settlement between Israel and Syria persuaded Arab oil producers to lift the embargo in March 1974. But OPAEC members, who would earn more than $100 billion in 1974 thanks to the price increases, now realized the enormous power they held with their ability to set oil prices by rationing its supply.

Crude oil prices over the next two decades fluctuated, notably in 1979 when the Shah of Iran was deposed, and again after Iraq's invasion of Kuwait in the 1990s. The energy crisis led to greater interest in renewable energy sources such as solar and wind power. Yet even now in the early 21st century, the world's dependence on Middle Eastern oil remains heavy.

There was also a political shift by many Western nations towards a pro-Arab approach that led to tensions in military alliances with the USA, which remained strongly pro-Israel. While the 1973 crisis had been averted, it was clear that the countries that controlled the oil fields would have much more of a say in the Middle East's political complexion in the years to come.

AT A GLANCE

October 1973's oil crisis – the six-month embargo placed on exports by the Arab petroleum exporting counties – had a massive effect on the USA and it's allies' infrastructure. Peace efforts in the Middle East saw the ban lifted, but the West would never again control oil prices, as the balance of power had changed irrevocably. And despite subsequent attempts to find alternative sources of energy, the West still relies on oil.

Self
Serve
Island
no smoking
Self
Serve
Island
no smoking
Self
Serve
Sorry . . .
Temporarily
out of
GASOLINE

Above: Nixon speaks with chief of staff H. R. Haldeman in the White House. Haldeman was later convicted for his role in Watergate.

Right: Richard Nixon departs in the Presidential helicopter from the south lawn of the White House on the day of his resignation.

NIXON RESIGNS

WASHINGTON, DC, USA
AUGUST 9, 1974

The Watergate Scandal in 1974 led to Richard Nixon becoming the first US president ever to resign from office, amidst a cloud of controversy. Watergate was a series of events that shocked the world and shook the USA to its foundations, fundamentally damaging that nation's faith in its political system.

The affair began in June 1972, when five men were caught breaking into the Democratic National Committee offices in the newly built Watergate complex in Washington DC. In January 1973, they were charged with conspiracy and burglary. All five, plus two others charged with assisting them, were found to have worked for agencies like the CIA, FBI and the US Marine Corps. Additionally, all seven were linked to the fundraising group Campaign to Re-elect the President, CRP, designed to keep Nixon in office.

Police investigations revealed the burglars were being bankrolled by the Nixon administration despite White House officials strenuously denying any involvement. Head of Nixon's re-election campaign John Mitchell had a fund to bankroll spying on Democratic activities, and the Watergate break-in was part of that. Two months later, in November 1972, Nixon was delighted to be re-elected President by a landslide majority.

But 1973 saw the net began to close around the Nixon administration. The US press – specifically the *New York Times* and *Washington Post* – highlighted the President's link to the break-in, dedicating many exclusive articles to the scandal with the help of a mystery informant known as 'Deep Throat'.

In April 1973, Nixon accepted the resignation of two of his closest aides, as well as Attorney General Richard Kleindienst. But efforts to cover up the break-in were blown apart at the committee hearings, when many of the recently departed aides implicated their former employers.

Key to their testimony was the claim that Nixon had recorded every conversation in his office since 1971. After a long battle, in which Nixon refused to hand over the tapes and even had independent prosecutor Archibald Cox dismissed, he was finally forced to hand them over, and he did this in July 1974.

The tapes exposed Nixon and his administration as being in league with the Watergate Five, and the Judiciary Committee recommended he be impeached for obstruction of justice, abuse of power and contempt of congress. Nixon, 61, resigned from office in August 1974, after a long drawn-out affair that tarnished not only the White House but the USA itself. He was granted a pardon by new president Gerald Ford, exempting him from prosecution, but he was a broken man.

AT A GLANCE

A June 1972 break-in at the Democratic National Committee offices led, two years later, to Richard Nixon becoming the first US President ever to resign from office after a series of lies and deceptions had failed to distance him from the crime. The nation's faith in its political system did not survive the trauma – and, despite a pardon from his successor, neither did Nixon's political career.

Above: Bill Gates and Paul Allen in 1983, after signing a contract to write MS-DOS for IBM. At that time, Microsoft had 100 employees.

Right: By 2005, Microsoft's main corporate campus in Seattle housed almost half of the company's 59,900 workers.

FOUNDING OF MICROSOFT

ALBUQUERQUE, NEW MEXICO, USA
1975

Founded by Bill Gates and Paul Allen in 1975, Microsoft expanded to become the third largest company on the planet, its products having helped create the personal computer (PC) as we know it, and with an estimated 500 million people around the globe using Microsoft products. Gates became the wealthiest man in the world.

Microsoft was founded in Albuquerque, New Mexico, after Gates had offered to produce a programming language system for an early computer known as the Altair 8800. Gates and Allen produced the program in weeks, and within five years the company was on its way to success. No industry was growing faster than computers, with technology progressing at a phenomenal rate, and Microsoft had arrived at the right time.

Their early years were spent providing their own computer operating system, MS-DOS, for hardware and software giant IBM, before Microsoft came into its own in 1983 with the release of its user-friendly word-processing program for a PC.

Word 1.0 was released in 1983, and the program changed the way the world used computers. It was a word processor that allowed the user to see what they were typing on the screen. After years of computers being a device that only trained operators could use, the user-friendly 'what you see is what you get' concept, with which Microsoft would become synonymous, opened up the PC to all.

Microsoft was now competing with other software companies like Macintosh and Corel, but then it began to leave its competitors behind. The first version of Windows was released in 1985, but it wasn't until Windows 3.0 five years later that Microsoft eclipsed its closest rival, Apple Macintosh. It went from strength to strength as the 20th century came to a close, constantly changing and becoming ever more complex with Windows 95, 98, and 2000. Now released on multiple platforms, Windows is claimed to be the number one computer operating system in the world.

Though Word and Windows are its two most successful products, Microsoft has been successful in other areas too; its Internet presence is characterized by its Internet Explorer browser, as well as the MSN network and Hotmail email system. In 2001 Microsoft branched into computer games consoles with the release of the X-Box. Since then it has released the console's successor, the X-Box 360, rivaling Sony's PlayStation.

From having just a handful of employees in New Mexico over three decades ago, Microsoft's expansionist marketing policy rocketed the company to the top, rewriting the way we use IT.

AT A GLANCE

The rise of Microsoft and the ubiquity of the personal computer went hand in hand. Its Windows operating system and Word word-processing package brought 'what you see is what you get' ease of operation to millions, making co-founder Bill Gates the world's wealthiest individual within less than a quarter of a century in business.

FALL OF SAIGON

SOUTH VIETNAM
APRIL 30, 1975

After over a century of conflict against a number of enemies, peace finally came to Vietnam: the fall of Saigon brought the end to the Vietnam War that had begun over 15 years earlier.

The battle for control of the country between the Republic of South Vietnam and the communist forces of North Vietnam had begun in 1959, with the USA heavily involved in accordance with their policy of communist containment.

But American support for US involvement in Vietnam had dwindled, leading to the withdrawal of its troops in 1973 after the signing of the Paris Peace Accords. Without the military support of its biggest ally, South Vietnam was now at a distinct disadvantage. The Watergate scandal had ousted President Nixon, and the new US government would not necessarily uphold the diplomatic assurances he had given to the South.

The US government said that they did not believe the South faced defeat, predicting they could hold out for at least a year. But in reality the South was on the ropes; a campaign of offensives from the North, named after communist icon and former president Ho Chi Minh, was going according to plan, and they were closing on the South's capital of Saigon.

The South's President Thieu resigned on April 21 after losing the confidence of his supporters. He was succeeded by Vice-President Tran Van Huong, who was himself replaced by Duong Van Minh six days later.

Minh had a less than a day in the hot seat before North Vietnamese troops stormed the outskirts of Saigon. As they continued to converge on the city, the USA, which had already been evacuating personnel since the beginning of the month, stepped up its efforts with Operation Frequent Wind, removing both US and South Vietnamese citizens thought to be at risk.

Saigon was in meltdown, with looting and rioting, and with its fall imminent Minh announced the South's surrender 'in order to avoid bloodshed' on April 30. Saigon was renamed Ho Chi Minh City. A year later, in July 1976, North and South Vietnam were reunified under communist rule, though April 30 has remained the national holiday.

It has taken decades for Vietnam to rebuild relations with other countries, even after the communist regime was relaxed in the eighties, but Ho Chi Minh City now appears as a sister city to beacons of modern capitalism like Lyon and San Francisco, a far cry from the capital of a defeated nation.

Above: North Vietnamese forces enter Saigon in 1975, completing the country's reunification.

Left: North Vietnamese troops seize the presidential palace in Saigon..

AT A GLANCE

The fall of Saigon, capital of South Vietnam, was inevitable from the moment, two years earlier, that President Nixon had withdrawn the US troops. The 15-year war came to an end having achieved little but loss of life (2,000,000 Vietnamese and 50,000 American), and the reunited country worked hard to rebuild relations with the outside world.

Above: An Apple 1 computer, sold in kit form in 1976 for $666.66. Steve Wozniak and friend Steve Jobs produced assembled boards for a local shop.

Right: John Sculley (left), President of Apple Computer, talks with Apple co-founders Steve Jobs (center) and Steve Wozniak (right) as they introduce a new Apple computer at a 1984 conference in San Francisco.

APPLE INC. IS FOUNDED

CUPERTINO, CALIFORNIA, USA

APRIL 1, 1976

Steven Jobs and Stephen Wosniak had been friends since 1971 when they were both working at Hewlett Packard. Wosniak was a self-taught electronics genius and by 1974, when Jobs was working as a technician at Atari, Wosniak had helped him design for the computer game *Breakout* an electronically efficient motherboard so tightly constructed that it could not be built by the assembly lines of the time.

In 1975 the two began to go to meetings of the Homebrew Computer Club in California. Wosniak was inspired by the latest generation of microcomputers to build his own, taking advantage of a cheap, newly available chip. When he demonstrated it at a Homebrew meeting, Jobs immediately saw the commercial potential of a pre-assembled motherboard and won 50 orders from their local computer store, The Byte Shop.

The motherboard complex, named Apple I, eventually sold around 200 copies. It had no keyboard or casing, but allowed hobbyists to use their TV as a monitor, and at $666.66, it gave the two Steves a healthy profit margin. They were able to give up their day jobs and concentrate on designing the Apple II, with better memory, graphics, a case and a keyboard.

The development of this more sophisticated Apple needed the sort of cash injection which Jobs and Wosniak, two college drop-outs, could not hope to attract alone. With the help of business angel Mike Markkula, they secured a bank loan of $250,000, and on April 1, 1976, Apple Inc. was born. They chose the name because it would be listed above the market leader Atari in the phone book.

The Apple II was released in 1977; it created and dominated the new home computer market, selling well into the 1980s. But the Apple III, designed to compete with the business market dominated by IBM, was less successful: it was prone to overheating and thousands were recalled.

It was the launch of the Apple Macintosh, with a 90-second commercial shown during the televised Superbowl XVIII in January 1984, which secured Apple's global status. Its new capacity for desktop publishing and computer animation made it the essential computer tool for the creative industries.

Both Jobs and Wosniak left Apple in the mid 1980s, Wosniak to pursue his interest in philanthropic work, teaching computer skills to schoolchildren, while Jobs bought and developed the cinema animation company Pixar. He returned to Apple in 1997, leading it into the new millennium with products such as the iMac and the ubiquitous iPod.

AT A GLANCE

Apple computers were at the forefront of bringing the personal computer into the homes of the world. Initially regarded as more expensive or elitist than the standard PC, Apple's range of products now includes phones and mobile music systems.

apple

FIRST TEST TUBE BABY IS BORN

OLDHAM GENERAL HOSPITAL, GREATER MANCHESTER, UK

JULY 25, 1978

When a child first looks up at their parents and asks, "How was I born?" the reply is sometimes an awkward one, the stork initially being the most popular answer amongst those who find the truth difficult. But when Louise Brown asked her parents the same question, the answer was completely different.

Louise was the world's first 'test tube baby', that is, conceived in a laboratory and transplanted into her mother's womb. She would be the first of well over a million worldwide in the years following her birth in July 1978. Her parents, Lesley and John Brown, were the first to undergo *in vitro* fertilization, IVF. Lesley's fallopian tubes were blocked and she was unable to conceive naturally despite a decade of attempts, but gynecologist Patrick Steptoe and physiologist Robert Edwards had a solution after rapid advances in procedures for the extraction of human eggs.

Steptoe and Edwards fertilized Lesley's egg with John's sperm in a laboratory and inserted it into her womb. Though Lesley developed toxemia during her pregnancy, it was otherwise uneventful and she was able to deliver Louise via a caesarean section on July 25.

Despite Louise being of low weight – just 5lb 12oz – her birth was a success. As the world's media gathered around Oldham General Hospital, Steptoe announced, "All examinations showed that the baby is quite normal. The mother's condition after delivery was also excellent."

Louise's birth opened the door to more births via IVF, including that of her younger sister Natalie; she was born four years later in 1982, by which point there had been 40 more test tube babies. (Natalie went on to become the first IVF baby to have a child herself, when in 1999, aged 17, she gave birth to her daughter naturally.)

Louise went on to have a normal childhood, and married in 2004. Two years later she had her own child; son Cameron arrived in 2006, also a natural conception. The advert for IVF treatment could not have been any better. And while the success rate remains below 20 per cent, the course still produces 'miracle' babies and offers hope to millions of couples who cannot conceive normally.

Above: Dr. Patrick Steptoe shows the suction device used to transplant a mature egg from the ovary of Mrs. Lesley Brown to a dish where it was fertilized with the sperm of her husband.

Left: Louise Brown, the world's first test tube baby, appears at age one on US television in 1979. Louise's mother Lesley holds her.

Below: Louise Brown, pictured with her parents in later life.

AT A GLANCE

With many women unable to conceive for gynecological reasons, the arrival of in vitro *fertilization in 1978 was truly an innovation that could potentially change lives. Louise Brown was the first of many test tube babies, conceived in a lab and born from her mother's womb.*

Above: Lech Walesa, pictured in front of a Solidarity banner in 1989, the year before he became Poland's president.

Right: Walesa is carried on the shoulders of a crowd in front of Warsaw's Supreme Court as Solidarity is recognized, 1980.

RECOGNITION OF SOLIDARITY BY THE POLISH GOVERNMENT

GDANSK, POLAND
AUGUST 30, 1980

The Solidarity (Solidarnosc) movement struck a strong blow for workers' rights when their charismatic leader, the mustachioed Lech Walesa, obtained the right for Polish trade unions to strike and to be independent. The deal was signed, most reluctantly, on the part of the communist government by the first deputy prime minister, Mieczyslaw Jagielski. By this agreement Poland became the first Eastern Bloc country to take such a step.

The key moment had come when around 17,000 Polish strikers had assembled in the Baltic shipyard in Gdansk, threatening to shut it down altogether. The catalyst for this upsurge had been a recent hike in food prices, but in fact the grievances were deep-rooted and based on longstanding social injustices. It was as a result of this demonstration that the agreement with the government was negotiated.

Lech Walesa, an unemployed electrician, was an unlikely leader, but he proved to be a good mouthpiece for the organization, mobilizing 20 other areas to join the strike. He became the undisputed leader of Solidarity, a national confederation of independent trade unions brought together under a single name.

The workers were promised, amongst other concessions, better social services, increased pay and more reliable food supplies. In return the government asked that the leading role of the communist party in Poland be acknowledged. This was no hardship for many Polish workers, who at that time were under the illusion that the communist party could be reformed from within.

It is impossible to exaggerate the feelings of excitement and hope that were felt as the news of these events was broadcast throughout the world. Very soon there were 9 million members of Solidarity. From the start, the Pope and the Polish Catholic church backed it to the hilt, sustaining popular support for the organization.

It could not last. the USSR was not slow to realize the importance of these events and put pressure on the Polish prime minister, General Jaruzelski, to act forcefully against the movement. In December 1981 he declared martial law, making Solidarity an illegal organization, and had its leaders arrested, including Lech Walesa; he spent almost a year in jail and was put under surveillance for the next seven years. Walesa's moment in the sun came in 1990, when he became Poland's president. But his success was short-lived; he eventually left the confederation, which declined steadily from then on.

AT A GLANCE

When the Polish government recognized Solidarity, acceding to demands for independent self-governing trade unions and the right to strike, it let loose powerful forces it could not control. It gave rise to hopes for freedom and a better future for workers. It also provided a stimulus for all who had believed, up to that point, that communist rule could not be challenged. Inevitably, the example of 'people power' in Poland inspired successful movements in other European countries, bringing many changes the political map of Eastern Europe.

FIRST COMMERCIALLY AVAILABLE CELLPHONE

USA

OCTOBER, 1983

It is hard to remember life without them, but it was only in 1983 that the first, brick-like cellphone was available to buy. Now, nearly three decades later, there are thousands of models used by millions of people the world over.

Above: An early 21st-century mobile phone, showing some of the applications available for them.

Left: Martin Cooper compares the Motorola DynaTAC phone, the world's first commercial handheld cellphone, with his current model during a news conference in 2009.

Portable telephone technology had been under development since the early 20th century, and included two-way radios and phones in vehicles that could latch onto networks. But the world at large relied on landlines and letters to communicate with far-off places. That is, until American telecoms giant Motorola emerged out front, to provide ordinary people with a portable handset they could buy themselves. It was the result of a race with fellow innovators AT&T and their Bell Laboratory, which had focused on portable communication through cars up to that point. But at Motorola, Martin Cooper led a team to create a device that could be hand-held, and used independently from a building or a vehicle.

Cooper made the first call from a cellphone a decade before its release, in 1973, using what would be known as the Motorola DynaTAC 8000X. It remained in development for a decade while a network was found from which it could operate, and the phone was released in October 1983.

It was far from perfect, however; and at a cost of over $3,000, only the rich could afford it. The handset itself was by today's standards large and bulky, at over ten inches long, and weighing nearly a kilogram (2.2 lbs).

Six years later Motorola followed up its success with the MicroTAC series, which saw the handset scaled down. The revolution had begun; by the end of the 20th century, second generation phones were widespread through manufacturers such as Sony and Nokia.

Rapidly advancing technology has meant cellphone capabilities have been greatly enhanced over the years. SMS messaging became a revolution in the 1990s when users could type messages instead of communicating through the spoken word.

The next step was the introduction of the Internet onto phone handsets in the first decade of the 21st century; cell phones had become much more than a simple communication device.

The call made by Martin Cooper over 30 years ago had lit the touch paper on the fastest evolving technology of the turn of the century. With an estimated 60 per cent of the planet's population now owning a cellphone, it is undoubtedly seen as one of the world's most essential accessories.

AT A GLANCE

It took two decades for the cellphone to slim down from the boxy prototype to the slim, pocket-friendly device we know today. Martin Cooper's vision in 1983 has revolutionized the way we communicate, making our arrangements on the move and sending messages at the tap of a keypad.

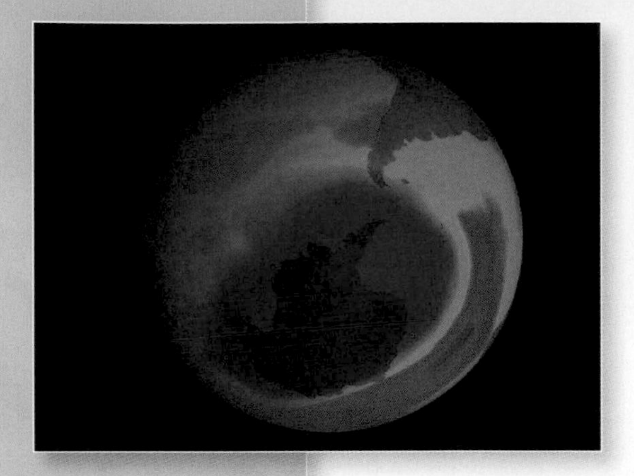

ALARM SOUNDS ON HOLE IN OZONE LAYER

ANTARCTICA
1985

For nearly a billion years the ozone layer has protected the Earth's surface from ultraviolet (UV) radiation. But a discovery in 1985 brought environmental issues into every political party's agenda for the coming decades – scientists discovered a hole in the ozone layer.

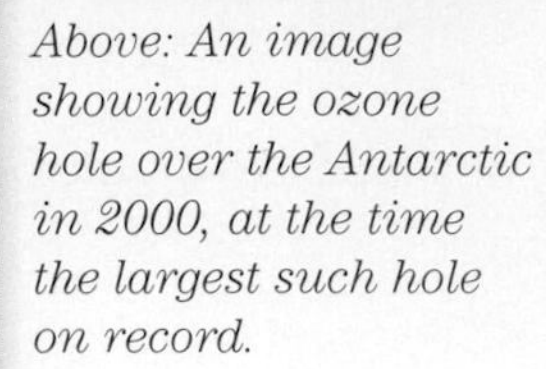

Above: An image showing the ozone hole over the Antarctic in 2000, at the time the largest such hole on record.

Left: French scientists launch a research balloon that will circle 20 km above Antarctica to inspect the ozone hole in the atmosphere.

In the 1970s research into the effects of certain chemicals and gases on the ozone layer around the Earth was in its infancy, but as it grew so did the recognized extent of the potential damage.

In 1985, British scientists Joseph Farman, Brian Gardiner and Jonathan Shanklin discovered that there was a substantial-sized gap in the protective ozone layer over the Antarctic during its spring months of September to December. This was due to the cold air causing man-made CFC gases to react with polar stratospheric clouds; when the tilt of the Earth means that the sun shines more directly onto the Antarctic, this causes the layer to degrade, creating a hole that can reach 1.5 times the size of the USA.

The revelation of this hole, coupled with the awareness of a worldwide decrease in the ozone layer estimated at four per cent per decade, changed the way the world thought. Environmental issues started to dominate news bulletins, and the press speculated about apocalyptic possibilities. In 1987, an international treaty was devised to prevent further damage to the ozone layer by limiting the amount of harmful gases created. The Montreal Protocol was signed in September that year, and implemented two years later, and was by all accounts considered a success.

The realization that the Earth is not indestructible has not only had an effect on environmental science and policies, but has also been reflected in our culture. Hollywood has capitalized on the subject's relevance and fear-provoking qualities with the release of environmental disaster movies like *The Day After Tomorrow* in 2004. The threat to the environment has also been coupled with the threat to humans; an increase in UV radiation leaves people at risk to cancer and other ailments, and this further heightened international concern.

As the noughties drew to a close, it was stated that the ozone hole was slowly reducing in size and was the smallest it had been in a decade. Even so, the planet's vulnerability had been exposed.

AT A GLANCE

The discovery by three British scientists in 1985 of a hole in the ozone layer over the Antarctic ensured environmental issues a place at the top of news agendas. Refrigerators and other users of the CFC gases that deplete ozone have been redesigned to reduce their environmental impact. The ozone hole is a different phenomenon from global warming, although there are links in their causes.

SEAL OF THE PRESIDENT OF THE UNITED STATES

Above: President Reagan and General Secretary Gorbachev together at the concluding summit ceremony at the International Press Center, Switzerland, 1985.

Left: General Secretary Mikhail Gorbachev stands at the podium with US President Ronald Reagan at a 1987 White House summit.

GORBACHEV ELECTED GENERAL SECRETARY OF THE SOVIET UNION

MOSCOW, USSR

MARCH 13, 1985

As the Soviet Union buried its third leader in less than three years, the baton of power was passed to a new generation, in the shape of 54-year-old Mikhail Gorbachev. The son of an agricultural mechanic on a collective farm, he was at the time the only Soviet leader to have been born after the October Revolution of 1917, and his election as General Secretary of the Communist Party of the Soviet Union signaled a new era. He would preside over the Soviet Union's final years, as his reforms inevitably led to the collapse of the old system.

Gorbachev led the funeral procession as his predecessor, Konstantin Chernenko, was buried near the Kremlin alongside fellow former leaders Leonid Brezhnev and Yuri Andropov. Gorbachev, the youngest man to take charge in Moscow since Stalin, immediately proposed a series of economic, political and cultural reforms including *glasnost* (openness), *perestroika* (restructuring), *demokratizatsiya* (democratization) and *uskoreniye* (acceleration of economic development), all launched in 1986 with the intention of making the Soviet economy more efficient.

He aimed to establish a free market economy by encouraging the private ownership of Soviet industry and agriculture – but existing structures ensured that these reforms were ineffective.

Gorbachev sent conciliatory messages to the West, confirming his wish to reduce arms stockpiles all round. He established a rapport with US President Ronald Reagan, British Prime Minister Margaret Thatcher and Germany's Chancellor Helmut Kohl, seeing improved international relations with them as a key to reform in his own country.

January 1986 saw him propose the elimination of intermediate range nuclear weapons in Europe, and in February 1988 he announced the full withdrawal of Soviet forces from Afghanistan – both moves at odds with past Soviet thinking. Then his publicly stated non-interference with the internal affairs of other countries allowed demonstrations to be made against communist governments in Eastern Europe without fear of reprisal, hastening the collapse of the communist bloc.

He was elected President of the Soviet Union in 1990, the same year in which his efforts toward ending the Cold War earned him the Nobel Peace Prize. But his attempts to make the Soviet Union a more democratic country made him unpopular with conservatives still in positions of power. Although in August 1991 he survived a coup staged by Communist party hard-liners, with the Soviet Union disintegrating into separate states he resigned later that year, ceding power to Boris Yeltsin.

AT A GLANCE

Mikhail Gorbachev tried to reform the stagnating communist party and the similarly moribund Soviet state economy by giving the people new freedoms. This, combined with improved relations with the West, inevitably led to the collapse of the Soviet Union. However, his concepts of glasnost *and* perestroika *are still remembered today.*

Above: *Thousands of fans pack Wembley Stadium for the 1985 Live Aid concert.*

Right: *Chrissie Hynde and Bob Geldof hold programs for the Live Aid concert.*

Overleaf: *A view from within the crowd of the stage during the Philadelphia Live Aid concert.*

AT A GLANCE

1985's Live Aid was the world's biggest ever charity rock concert, aimed to raise money for the relief of famine in the Sudan and Ethiopia. It was the idea of Irish rock star Bob Geldof. 50 acts appeared in London and Philadelphia, the music transmitted worldwide via satellite. An estimated £150 million was raised.

LIVE AID CONCERT

WEMBLEY ARENA, LONDON AND JFK STADIUM, PHILADELPHIA

JULY 13, 1985

The power of rock music and television came together in 1985 to create a showbiz spectacle designed to raise money for African famine relief. Fifty of the biggest names in music including Queen, Paul McCartney, Madonna and U2, plus a re-formed Led Zeppelin, performed for a global audience reached through satellite transmission. There had been one-off charity concerts before, like George Harrison's Concert for Bangladesh in 1971, but Live Aid eclipsed all-comers in reach and ambition, setting a template for future events.

The concert followed the1984 charity single 'Do They Know It's Christmas?' recorded by Bob Geldof (Boomtown Rats) and Midge Ure (Ultravox) with a galaxy of UK pop stars under the name Band Aid. Geldof had been touched by a BBC news report of the famine in Ethiopia and wanted to make a gesture. When the record sold three million copies, it was clear the public had taken the cause to heart.

USA for Africa's single 'We Are The World' followed suit, but a visit to Africa convinced Geldof that a greater effort was needed. Live Aid was conceived in March 1985 and organised in just 20 weeks. As well as the concert itself, the means to dispense the proceeds had also to be created – a yet bigger challenge.

Geldof's relentless harrying of the era's biggest stars ensured few turned him down. From Adam Ant to Neil Young, the Beach Boys to the Who (who re-formed for the event), the A-Z of pop was represented. Springsteen, Prince and Michael Jackson were the most notable absentees. Throughout the concerts, TV viewers were urged to donate money to the Live Aid cause – often by Geldof himself, whose on-air use of the f-word when disappointed by the amount thus far raised increased giving to £300 per second.

Each act was given just 15 minutes to perform at Wembley Stadium in London and JFK Stadium, Philadelphia; New York's Shea Stadium, the first-choice American venue, was unavailable. Phil Collins flew by Concorde to play on both sides of the Atlantic. While 72,000 people attended in London and 99,000 in Philadelphia, the TV audience amounted to an estimated 400 million viewers across 60 countries thanks to an unprecedented global link-up.

One of the organisers later put the final figure raised as £150 million ($284 million), far more than the originally hoped-for £1 million. Irish-born Geldof received a knighthood from Queen Elizabeth II in 1986 in recognition of his work. In 2005, Sir Bob Geldof marked the 20th anniversary with Live 8, a series of global concerts intended to persuade leaders of the G8 countries to 'make poverty history'.

WORLD-WIDE CONCERT BOOK
LIVE AID
INTRODUCTION BY
BOB GELDOF
BE A PART OF THE INTERNATIONAL EFFORT TO SAVE LIVES
ALL PUBLISHER'S PROFITS FROM THE SALE OF THIS BOOK WILL BE USED FOR AFRICAN FAMINE RELIEF

LIVE
AID
AT&T
PEPSI
THE CHOICE OF A
NEW GENERATION

LIVE
AID

FALL OF THE BERLIN WALL

BERLIN
NOVEMBER 9, 1989

The Berlin Wall was a stark reminder of the division between communism and capitalism that had split Europe after the end of World War II. The defeat of Hitler led to Germany being partitioned into East and West, the former under communist rule. The city of Berlin, situated deep in the new East Germany, was also partitioned, with the US, Britain, France and the Soviet Union each controlling a zone; as with the country, this arrangement became East and West Berlin.

Above: *A traffic jam at Checkpoint Charlie after the opening of the Berlin Wall.*

Left: Man attacks the Berlin Wall with a pickaxe on the night of November 9th.

The 28-mile-long Wall, built in 1961 at the bidding of German Democratic Republic leader Walter Ulbricht, became a stark reminder of the division between communism and capitalism. The Wall succeeded in stemming the steady flow of refugees from East to West, estimated at 2.5 million in the years since 1949 – but there were still those desperate enough to try; between 1962 and 1989 some 5,000 succeeded, and an estimated 100 lost their lives in the attempt.

The year before the Wall's fall in 1989 had seen Soviet leader Mikhail Gorbachev announce a unilateral cut in weapons levels in Eastern Europe – a reduction of half a million troops and 10,000 tanks. This followed a passionate speech in 1987 given by US President Ronald Reagan at the Brandenburg gate urging his Russian counterpart to 'tear down this Wall'.

Mass demonstrations in East Germany had led to the resignation of Erich Honeker, and this groundswell of public opinion was the immediate prelude to the fall of the Berlin Wall. On November 9, new GDR leader Egon Krentz opened the crossing points, and the once seemingly impregnable barrier became a site of rejoicing as separated families poured through the gates for joyful reconciliations.

In the first two days, over a million East Berliners took advantage of the new freedom to visit the West. And when, the following July, former Pink Floyd musician Roger Waters staged a performance of 'The Wall' in the nearby Potsdamer Platz, his special guests, German rock band the Scorpions, were inspired to write 'Wind Of Change' in honour of the event.

Souvenir hunters ensured the hated Wall was soon dismantled, and by the first anniversary only three short sections remained as a reminder of Berlin's divided past. On 3 October 1990, Berlin became the German capital once more. The reintegration of East and West Germany, with their markedly differing levels of economic prosperity, as the Federal Republic of Germany would prove rather more difficult, and the process is still ongoing.

AT A GLANCE

The Berlin Wall divided Germany's former capital between 1961 and 1989, dividing families and causing over 100 fatalities as would-be escapees were shot by East German border guards. When a new spirit of liberalism provoked by mass demonstrations convinced East Germany's leaders that partition was now impractical, the crossing points were opened, and the following year both city and country were officially reunited in the Federal Republic of Germany.

Above: Mandela's freedom is demanded by South Africans in a demonstration the year before his release.

Right: Nelson Mandela and his then wife Winnie, moments after his release from Victor Verster prison in February 1990.

Below: Removing graffiti from a wall of King's College Chapel, in Cambridge, UK, in 1965.

NELSON MANDELA RELEASED FROM PRISON

PAARL, SOUTH AFRICA
FEBRUARY 11, 1990

South Africa was a country that had been divided by racial issues for over 100 years, and the introduction of apartheid (complete racial segregation) in 1948 by the country's government cast a deeper shadow over the country for nearly 50 years.

One victim was 46-year-old Nelson Mandela, jailed for life in 1964 for planning to sabotage the administration and the country's economy with his party, the African National Congress (ANC). His release 27 years later would signal the end of apartheid in that country.

Under the existing regime, racial segregation had been legal for many years, and Afrikaners – white Africans of European descent – enjoyed minority rule. Mandela and his party spent the 1940s and 1950s attempting to fight for equality and derail the system. But the government banned the ANC party. Mandela was a believer in non-violent resistance, inspired by Indian independence pioneer Mahatma Gandhi, but he changed his views after the Sharpeville massacre of 1960, in which nearly 70 peacefully protesting black Africans were shot dead by police. Having been acquitted of treason in 1956, Mandela was convicted eight years later and jailed for life.

He spent the majority of the time incarcerated in Robben Island prison. Whilst he was inside, apartheid continued to hold sway, but the resistance movement was gathering pace; Mandela's imprisonment meant he was seen as a figurehead in the struggle, and his reputation grew apace.

He was moved to Pollsmoor prison in 1982, home to some of South Africa's most dangerous criminals, before being transferred to the low-security Victor Verster prison. Pressure for his release was now mounting in both Africa and further afield, and this appeared a very real possibility when President Pieter Willem Botha suffered a stroke and was forced to resign from office. His replacement was National Party leader Frederik Willem de Klerk, who immediately began dismantling the apartheid regime, lifting the ban on the ANC. Six months after taking office, he released Nelson Mandela.

Mandela, 71, walked free on February 11, 1990, just days after de Klerk lifted the bans on the ANC and other anti-apartheid groups. Mandela emerged to address a crowd of thousands, and pledged to continue his people's fight for freedom.

Mandela and de Klerk contested the country's first multi-racial democratic election in 1994, with the ANC triumphing and Mandela being elected the country's first black president. It was a turnaround that few had thought possible just a few years earlier, the result of half a decade of struggle.

AT A GLANCE

Jailed African National Congress leader Nelson Mandela had become the figurehead of the opposition to South Africa's apartheid system. His release after 27 years signaled the overthrow of apartheid and the country's first free elections, after which he became South Africa's first black president. He stepped down in 1999.

Semantic
Web

Above: Left to right, Internet pioneers Vinton Cerfy, Lawrence Roberts, Robert Kahn and Tim Berners-Lee, after jointly winning the 2002 Prince of Asturias Award for Scientific and Technological Research.

Left: Tim Berners-Lee, inventor of the World Wide Web, stands at a chalkboard on which he has written notes on Web development.

INVENTION OF THE WORLD WIDE WEB

SWITZERLAND

1991

While many people think the World Wide Web is the Internet, many do not realize that they are separate entities, though without the Web the Internet would never have evolved the way it has.

The Web was the brainchild of British physicist and computer scientist Tim Berners-Lee, who realized that the growing technology of the Internet needed a public interface in order to expand and become user-friendly. The idea of the Internet as a 'network of networks' had been around for decades, though it had not yet reached mainstream awareness.

Berners-Lee was working at the European Council for Nuclear Research (CERN) in Switzerland when he first proposed the idea of 'a large hypertext database with typed links' – that is, a way of connecting the many pages of information in a network through links that can be read both by humans and by computers. It was a simple idea that gave the world a way of presenting and sharing data through the Internet.

His ideas converged with those of a fellow worker, Belgian Robert Cailliau, and together they created the names and all the relevant protocols that we take for granted today, such as html to format a page, and http to travel between them. Their initial aim was to make it easier for their colleagues to access information on company computers, but it was rapidly becoming much more than that.

Student Nicola Pellow adapted the Web system to run on any computer, and soon software was developed through which to view the Internet. Early developmental browsers preceded market leaders like Mosaic and later Netscape, before Microsoft's Internet Explorer became the number one way to view the Internet. The Web was snowballing, and websites were popping up all over the Internet.

Fast forward just one decade, and the Web had created countless businesses and revolutionized the Internet in ways that in its infancy were unimaginable to most of us. We now have things we take for granted like searching for information at a touch of a button through Google, or buying practically anything we can think of through online shopping sites such as ebay and Amazon.com.

In December 2009 there were an estimated 233 million websites on the Web, and if a company or even an individual doesn't have an online presence they are considered to be behind the times. The Web has changed the way the planet works, and it has never seemed smaller.

AT A GLANCE

The arrival of the World Wide Web in 1991 made the Internet a user-friendly phenomenon. Created by Briton Tim Berners-Lee, it turned the chaos of online communication into order, allowing users to click links and explore cyberspace in a logical manner. Thanks to the Web, the world shrank in a matter of years.

Above: Bezos announces the Kindle 2 electronic reader, a device that now permits Amazon to sell electronic or e-books.

Right: Amazon.com founder Jeff Bezos poses in his Seattle headquarters three years after launching the Internet bookstore.

FOUNDING OF AMAZON.COM

NEW YORK, USA
1994

Only a few years after the invention of the World Wide Web, the Internet was growing fast, and many people were jumping onto the bandwagon during the dot-com boom. It was in 1995 that the retail site Amazon.com was founded. It's now the number one choice when buying online, but it wasn't always that way.

Jeff Bezos worked as an analyst for New York-based firm D. E. Shaw & Co after his graduation from Princeton University. While at work, he began looking for gaps in the rapidly expanding market of the Internet. He came up with the idea of Amazon, which he originally planned to be an online bookstore.

He chose books, as opposed to a mail order catalogue, due to the sheer volume of listings he could store online. He was realistic about the chances of failure in an unproven industry, but realized he couldn't let the chance pass. "It was like the wild, wild West, a new frontier. And I knew that if I didn't try this, I would regret it. And that would be inescapable."

The company's early days were characterized by rapid growth but an even faster-growing uncertainty, as the venture was making heavy losses – by the early noughties its share prices had plummeted and staff were being made redundant. This, despite Amazon adding much more than books to its repertoire; in its first five years it had expanded from books to CDs, electronics and similar consumer goodies, toys and home improvement goods.

In the face of extreme adversity and near-certain closure, Amazon made its first profit towards the end of 2001 – the faith in it had paid off. In the years that it had been hemorrhaging money, it had been expanding at such a rate online that other companies could not keep up; in retrospect it was only a matter of time until it turned a profit. Amazon had become the number one e-commerce business on the planet.

Amazon is not only the USA's largest online retailer but the biggest in the world, selling goods from books to electronics to jewelry. It is also a story of perseverance in the dot-com industry where although success may look inevitable it is far from guaranteed.

AT A GLANCE

From its inception in 1994 as an online bookstore, Amazon has become the best known one-stop solution for Internet shopping. Jeff Bezos' creation survived its loss-making early years to become a household name, one that will very likely continue to serve millions worldwide for years to come.

MATH FOR EVERY KID
Why I Am Not a Christian Bertrand Russell
Exit, Voice, and Loyalty
Hirschman
1997
Epstein Mirza
1997
Epstein Mirza
ART
A HISTORY OF ANCIENT EGYPT
NICOLAS GRIMAL
ORIGINAL PRONOUNCEMENTS ACCOUNTING STANDARDS AS OF JUNE 1, 1996
THE BODY LANGUAGE AND EMOTION OF CATS
Danny Goodman JavaScript BIBLE Second Edition
Danny Goodman JavaScript BIBLE Second Edition
Danny Goodman JavaScript BIBLE Second Edition
GLOBAL ADVANTAGE on the INTERNET
THE BOOK OF THE SWORD
Burton
Dover
YOGA
The Spirit and Practice of Moving into Stillness
Erich Schiffmann
Access 97 for Dummies
ACUPRESSURE FOR LOVERS
MAPPLETHORPE

Above: The world's press is introduced to Dolly in 1997, the year after her successful cloning.

Right: Dolly, the world's first cloned sheep, at age two at the Roslin Institute in Edinburgh, Scotland

FIRST CLONED SHEEP

EDINBURGH, SCOTLAND

JULY 5, 1996

In July 1996, experimenters cloned the first animal. Rather than call the creation Frankenstein or something equally horrifying, they named her the rather placid Dolly after country and western singer Dolly Parton; the quick-witted stockmen who had attended the delivery made the link between the busty singer and the mammary gland that had been used to clone the sheep.

Dolly was the only lamb that survived to adulthood from 277 attempts at somatic cell nuclear transfer, a technique where the nucleus from an adult cell is transferred into an unfertilized developing egg cell from which the nucleus had been removed. Most embryos created this way and implanted in a surrogate proved to have defects, and were terminated. Dolly's birth was kept under wraps for nearly a year, because while it would be heralded a scientific miracle it would also spark controversy and heated debates over the ethics of the procedure. True to form, the world reacted with both awe and disgust when Dolly's existence became known in 1997.

It was not the first time scientists at the Roslin Institute in Midlothian, Scotland, had attempted a live animal clone, but the success of Dolly's case led to international debate. When the head of the team who created the sheep hinted that the technique might be viable for human cloning, the media went into overdrive.

During her lifetime, Dolly gave birth to six offspring after being regularly mated with a Welsh mountain ram. This brought yet more attention to the already infamous ewe.

Then, at five years old, Dolly was spotted walking stiffly; tests confirmed she was suffering from arthritis, unusual at such a young age. Debate once again raged over the ethics of cloning and the possibility of an advanced aging process; Dolly was rumored to have the body of a six-year-old at birth, the same age as the sheep she was cloned from. The arthritis was a blow, but was controlled – but when another cloned sheep died from a lung disease it was considered likely Dolly might suffer the same fate. Sure enough, tumors were discovered in 2003, and it was decided that she should not continue to suffer.

Dolly's creation was a scientific breakthrough, and captured the public's imagination. Soon wild theories starting flying around of Jurassic Park-style dinosaurs roaming the earth and deceased loved ones being cloned after their death. It was the merging of science fiction and reality, despite the ongoing feud about the ethics behind it. Dolly really was 'the world's most famous sheep'.

AT A GLANCE

The creation of Dolly, a sheep created from cloned embryonic cells, created a storm in the world's press when it was announced in 1997, a year after her birth. While horses and bulls have since been cloned, Dolly's arrival did not herald a 'brave new world' of mutant and/or previously extinct animals, and the sheep herself only survived to the age of six.

1961 – 1997

DEATH OF PRINCESS DIANA

PARIS, FRANCE
AUGUST 31, 1997

Diana, Princess of Wales, had been a much-needed shot in the arm for the British royal family since her marriage to Charles, Prince of Wales, in July 1981. She was a young, vibrant and relevant member of the monarchy whose charity work drew admiration from many, as did the way she conducted herself in a family that some were saying was out of touch with the public. A nation mourned in August 1997, when news came through of her untimely death in Paris.

Above: Diana, Princess of Wales, on a royal visit in 1983 as she would forever be remembered.

Left: Floral tributes left outside Kensington Palace after the death of Diana, Princess of Wales.

Inset: The tunnel in Paris where Princess Diana met her death in a 1997 auto accident.

Diana, her partner Dodi Fayed, her bodyguard Trevor Rees-Jones, and driver Henri Paul, were involved in a car crash in Paris while fleeing paparazzi photographers. Everyone except Rees-Jones died as the car, having entered the Pont de l'Alma tunnel, struck a supporting pillar at an estimated 65 mph.

Diana had long been a target for the international media, her youth, looks and royal status making her a regular on newspaper front pages worldwide. The princess had graced those pages even more often than usual in the years leading up to her death, as after years of marital issues she and Prince Charles had separated in late 1992 and divorced four years later. Both had admitted adultery.

In the summer of 1997, Diana began dating Dodi, son of Harrods owner and Fulham Football Club chairman Mohamed Fayed. Diana and Dodi embarked on a romance which was highly publicized, as was inevitable with the Princess. After a holiday on the Fayed family yacht in the Italian and French Rivieras, they stopped off in Paris en route to London. They stayed at the Ritz Hotel, owned by Dodi's father, before heading out towards an apartment near the Champs Elysées.

As they set off in a blacked-out Mercedes, they were tailed by a number of paparazzi; as the car entered the tunnel the driver lost control and crashed into a pillar. Diana was taken to hospital but died a few hours later. It was later discovered the driver had consumed both drugs and alcohol before getting behind the wheel; he was blamed for the crash by a subsequent judicial investigation.

A nation poured out its grief as tens of thousands lined the streets of London, and over 30 million people watched the funeral on television, along with millions more across the world. At the service Elton John's rewritten version of 'Candle in the Wind' proclaimed, 'Goodbye England's Rose.' Though Diana had been a controversial figure in many ways, her impact on Britain, both in life and in death, has been undeniable.

AT A GLANCE

Diana, the People's Princess, lived a highly public life, but showed a common touch that endeared her to millions and deflected much criticism from the British royal family. Her death in Paris in 1997 has since been the subject of conspiracy theories, but was found to be a tragic accident due to negligent driving and the pursuing press pack.

Overleaf: Guardsmen of the Prince of Wales Company of the Welsh Guards attend the casket along the route of the funeral procession of Diana, Princess of Wales.

Declines
3965
Nasdaq
3294.97 -381.8
2,301,025,454
Daily Value
Nasdaq
3294.97 -381.8
2,301,025,454
4055.9
3769.63
-14.1%
1752.30
33 9/16
1818.8

DOT-COM BUBBLE BURSTS

NEW YORK STOCK EXCHANGE, USA

MARCH 10, 2000

Inset: High-tech workers, unemployed and job-hunters, networking at a dot-com 'pink slip' party in February 2001; these parties, held to help people find new jobs, first came about following the huge job losses that happened when the dot-com bubble burst.

Left: Dismay at the New York Stock Exchange as the NASDAQ tumbles through April 2000.

At the approach of the 21st century, the Internet and the World Wide Web were thriving. The computer-based technology was coming into its own, with continually developing equipment creating many commercial opportunities to market products and services.

The emergence of online companies began apace, and their rapid arrival sparked a period of on-paper prosperity that would become known as the 'dot-com bubble'. Eventually that bubble would burst, with disastrous consequences.

The far-reaching ability of the Internet, along with its rapidly increasing audience, made it an attractive proposition for existing companies to expand and for new ones to form. The entrepreneurs who formed these companies did so by collaborating with venture capitalists – financial benefactors who had the resources to get the new ventures up and running.

There was no shortage of willing investors, as the general feeling was that the Internet was the future, and any foray into it would reap large financial rewards. These companies operated on the premise that to gain success they needed to 'get big quick', expanding their customer base very rapidly even if it meant trading at a loss for the time being. Though in retrospect this seems like a fundamentally flawed business plan, it ended up working well for a few enterprises, most notably Amazon.com.

Many of the dot-com companies entered the stock market to became publicly traded, even those with little to no history and who had turned no profit. Such was the optimism around these new companies then that their stocks rose dramatically and they became overvalued. The peak came on March 10, 2000; the US stock market, NASDAQ, closed at an astronomically high 5,048.62. The companies and their investors were very rich – on paper. But the only way out of this crazy situation was down; a four per cent drop the next day was the beginning of mass panic selling that signaled the end of the dot-com bubble.

Many businesses went bust in the years following, and many individuals were left with a lot less money than before. The incident proved yet again that in business caution is sometimes the best way to proceed. The Internet continued to flourish regardless, and is now the number one technological medium in the world – but a lot of its early companies did not stay afloat to see it.

AT A GLANCE

The modern equivalent of historical boom'n'busts such as the South Sea Bubble and the Gold Rush, the dot-com bubble was the result of investors being seduced by the advent of the Internet and overestimating its ability to turn everything it touched into gold. The inevitable result was a crash, sorting the well run ventures able to deliver on their promises from those launched on a wing and a prayer.

ENRON INVESTIGATION BEGINS

HOUSTON, TEXAS, USA
OCTOBER 22, 2001

Above: Former Enron CEO Kenneth Lay, who cited his Fifth Amendment rights and refused to testify during a Congressional hearing into his company's demise.

Left: Enron Vice President of Corporate Development Sherron Watkins testifies at the Enron Senate hearing.

When the energy company Enron collapsed in late 2001, it revealed a rotten, corrupt financial structure behind the illusory façade of all-American corporate success. In February that year it had been paying its executives million-dollar bonuses and advising the White House on energy policy, having been named Most Innovative Company in America for the sixth year running. But by Christmas it was bankrupt and under investigation by the US Securities and Exchange Commission.

What lay behind the glamorous veneer of multinational expansion and spectacular profit levels was a fraudulent accounting system which concealed losses in artificial subsidiaries. Enron deliberately misled shareholders into the belief that the company could deliver good returns on their investment, ensuring that money would continue to flow into the company – and into the pockets of its executives.

From its 1930s origins as a gas distribution company, Enron suddenly grew in the mid-1980s when Kenneth Lay became its CEO. He expanded the corporation's interests and overstretched its capacity with questionable dealings, covering up the resulting business failures with some fairly ruthless 'creative accounting'.

In 1990 he was joined at Enron by Jeff Skilling, from the failed First City Bank of Houston, and Andrew Fastow from the failed Commercial Bank of Illinois. The three men bought and created a multinational maze of interdependent companies amongst which they hid debts and exaggerated profits. They created a business culture at the company's Houston headquarters in which its directors and accountants went along with the trio's dubious practices, tolerating the sometimes illegal conflicts of interest instead of challenging them.

In August 2001, however, Sherron Watkins, vice president for corporate development at Enron, began to voice concerns about its accounting systems. She had formerly worked at Arthur Anderson, Enron's accountants, and knew what she was talking about. Her questions to Kenneth Lay triggered quiet panic in the offices of both Enron and its accountants, leading to executives ditching share holdings and Arthur Anderson shredding documents while insisting that Enron was in robust good health.

But the façade crumbled, and on December 2, Enron became the largest corporate bankruptcy in American history. Arthur Anderson, one of the five largest accounting firms in the world at the time, also collapsed. Skilling was sentenced to 24 years for felony. Fastow, convicted of fraud, money laundering and conspiracy, reduced his sentence by turning state evidence. Lay was convicted on ten counts but died of a heart attack before being sentenced. Watkins now speaks at conferences on the dangers of US corporate culture.

AT A GLANCE

The rise and fall of Enron exposed how accounting could be used to cover up corporate malpractice, deceiving regulators and shareholders and diverting money into the pockets of executives. Enron's bankruptcy in 2001 was the curtain-raiser to the most volatile decade in world business since the Great Depression.

HURRICANE KATRINA

NEW ORLEANS, USA
AUGUST 2005

Above: An abandoned house three months after Hurricane Katrina hit the Lower Ninth Ward of the city of New Orleans.

Right: A US Army loadmaster surveys a flooded New Orleans from his Chinook helicopter.

Below: Evacuees take shelter from the elements in the giant Houston Astrodome sports arena.

In August 2005 the US state of Louisiana was devastated by Hurricane Katrina. The week-long tropical cyclone became the biggest natural disaster in the history of the USA, causing damage estimated at over $80 billion.

The Atlantic hurricane season usually peaks in the northern hemisphere's late summer, September the most active month. The 2004 season had resulted in over 3,000 deaths and caused nearly $50 billion worth of damage, and many people in Louisiana and the surrounding states were bracing themselves for a repeat.

Katrina began on August 23 as a tropical depression just south of the Bahamas with winds of 35 mph, but it quickly escalated and clipped the coast of Florida by August 25, with winds peaking at 75 mph. In its brief journey through Florida, Katrina caused 14 deaths and left millions of people without electricity.

It was a sign of things to come. As Katrina crossed the Gulf of Mexico it became a Category 5 hurricane, intensifying with winds of 175 mph. By now the states of Louisiana and Mississippi were on the alert for the impending storm, with a mandatory evacuation ordered for the city of New Orleans.

Katrina reached land again as a Category 3 on August 29, hitting Buras-Triumph, Louisiana. The town was no stranger to hurricanes, having been heavily damaged four times already in the last century, the most recent experience having come 35 years previously with Hurricane Camille.

Sited below sea level, New Orleans was predicted to be in a catastrophic situation, as it was thought the strength of the storm would breach the city's system of levees, raised banks built to keep the water at bay. The levees and floodwalls did indeed prove grossly ineffective; Katrina left an estimated 80 per cent of the city submerged in its wake.

Destruction was severe, and while the evacuation of the city was considered a success by and large, many people – mainly the poor and the elderly – stayed behind. Buildings were destroyed, and nearly 1,500 died. The city descended into chaos, with no clean water, electricity or shelter. Shops and buildings were looted, and many residents congregated at the city's Superdome stadium, which quickly became overcrowded and filthy.

Reconstruction of New Orleans was painfully slow, and two years after Katrina, areas of it were still uninhabitable. In 2007 the city was estimated to have regained 60 per cent of its pre-hurricane population, and it was clear that the path of destruction left by Hurricane Katrina would take many years to be fully erased.

AT A GLANCE

The natural disaster of Hurricane Katrina saw the residents of New Orleans pay the price for living below sea level. The levee system designed to hold back the surrounding sea could not cope with hurricane-force winds, and there was widespread damage. President Bush's response to the disaster was widely criticized as too little too late, and five years later the city had still not returned to its pre-Katrina state.

E PLURIBUS
UNUM
DEER PARK
MR. MUDD

FEDERAL TAKEOVER OF FANNIE MAE AND FREDDIE MAC

WASHINGTON, DC, USA
SEPTEMBER 7, 2008

Fannie Mae and Freddie Mac were early casualties in a chain of crises amongst financial institutions that triggered a global economic recession. In their collapse they exposed all the risks of the property market boom of the early years of the 21st century.

Above: The Washington headquarters of mortgage lender Fannie Mae, taken over by the US government in 2008 after bad debt problems had proved insurmountable.

Left: Former Freddie Mac and Fannie Mae CEOs are sworn in before the House Committee examining the extent to which their corporations' actions and policies may have contributed to the mortgage crisis.

Fannie Mae, more properly the Federal National Mortgage Association, and Freddie Mac, the Federal Home Loan Mortgage Corporation, acted as mortgage brokers to the subprime market – that is, clients with a less than prime, or good, credit rating. It is by definition a high-risk market, consisting of vulnerable people which the two organizations had originally been established to serve and protect.

Deregulation and political pressure around the turn of the century, under Presidents Clinton and Bush, undermined much of that protection. Unscrupulous lenders were able to offer deceptively low initial rates to the poorest members of society, inducing them to acquire debts which they could not afford to repay, especially when the housing bubble burst in 2006.

The proportion of subprime borrowers defaulting on their loans rose to one in four in early 2008. Thousands of homes were repossessed; house prices fell, and those who now owned these repossessed buildings found that their assets were worthless. Fannie Mae and Freddie Mac handled about half the mortgages in the USA, worth $5 trillion in mortgage-backed securities, and now faced combined debts of around $1.6 trillion.

The US government's move to take over the running of Mae and Mac in September was an unprecedented intervention in a country characterized by relatively unregulated, hands-off capitalism. The action sought to stabilize the housing market; but financial institutions all over the world had a finger in the property pie, and when confidence in that collapsed then so did they. In Britain, the Northern Rock bank had already been rescued by the government in February 2008, and other British banks were effectively nationalized a month after the US intervention. Banks everywhere restricted credit, and businesses large and small found themselves unable to operate. As many high-profile high street names were declared bankrupt, unemployment rose and spending fell. By the start of 2009, much of the world was deep in recession.

Although by the end of 2009 the world had emerged from the darkest phase, full recovery would, it became clear, take much longer. Those governments, institutions and businesses which had survived the recession must now count the cost, erase deficits and try to recoup their losses; belts must remain tightened for years to come.

AT A GLANCE

The failure of the US subprime mortgage market in which Fannie Mae and Freddie Mac were the major players had a knock-on effect that was felt worldwide. The American government moved to take them over, while similar nationalisation of overexposed banks took place in Britain as a worldwide recession loomed.

Above: Barack Obama on his way to be sworn in as the 44th President of the United States.

Right: Supporters of Barack Obama celebrate in Chicago as he wins the presidential election.

Overleaf: Thousands look on as Barack Obama takes the Oath of Office as the 44th President of the United States, sworn in by US Chief Justice John Roberts.

PRESIDENT BARACK OBAMA ELECTED

USA

NOVEMBER 4, 2008

When the United States of America elected Barack Obama as their 44th president, it was a historic moment for a country whose history had been peppered with racial prejudice, violence and the long fight for civil rights.

The early to mid 20th century in America had been a period fraught with tension between whites and their black counterparts, characterized by segregation and the campaign for racial equality led by iconic figures such as Martin Luther King Jr. At that time, the thought of a black man being elected leader of the country would have been unthinkable, but 44 years after the Civil Rights Act of 1964, it happened.

Barack Obama was born in 1961 in Honolulu, Hawaii, to a white mother and a black father. His parents divorced in 1964, and Obama spent part of his early childhood in Indonesia with his mother's new husband. He moved to Los Angeles as an 18-year-old, before studying in New York City, and later Harvard Law School.

After a brief spell as a civil rights attorney he entered the political realm in 1996. He began as Senator of Illinois, before becoming a US Senator in 2005. He was already making waves, and was spoken of as a potential Democratic presidential candidate.

Obama threw his hat into the ring for the presidential election in early 2007. With the desire for change prevalent throughout the country after eight years of President George Bush and his Republican party, Obama was seen as a favorite from the beginning; hopes were high for a new party and new figurehead at the helm.

It did not bode well for his opponent, Republican and former Vietnam prisoner of war John McCain. When the two Senators went head to head, calling on the country for their votes, the result was the highest voting election for four decades, with at least 130 million Americans having their say.

November 4, 2008, was results day, and it was Obama who triumphed, with a 52.3 per cent share of the popular vote. He finished with 365 Electoral College votes to McCain's 173, after taking eight previously Republican states, among them Florida and Indiana.

As he addressed his home state of Illinois after his historic victory, Obama proclaimed, "It's been a long time coming, but tonight change has come to America." Indeed it had – a new face and a new era for a country that was beginning to emerge from the shadow of its past.

AT A GLANCE

With its history of institutionalized racism, the likelihood of the USA ever having a black president was considered a pipe dream by many. But Hawaiian-born Barack Obama proved in the 2008 presidential election that the American dream was indeed open to anyone at last, no matter what their color.

CNN POLITICS
CNN PROJECTION
BARACK OBAMA
ELECTED PRESIDENT
CNN
LIVE
CALIFORNIA
PRESIDENT
55
MCCAIN
0%
OBAMA
0%
0% CNN PROJECTION
MCCAIN
139
OBAMA
297

GAME OVER
Mubarak

ارحل يا فرعون
مطلب من
ارحل يا مبارك

Above: Survivors look at a leisure boat balanced on top of a house in the tsunami devastated port of Otsuchi city in Iwatei, Prefecture.

Right: The tsunami engulfed a residential area in Natori, Miyagi Prefecture, northeastern Japan.

Overleaf: A solitary tsunami survivor weeps in tears amid debris in the devastated town of Natori, Miyagi prefecture, Japan.

JAPANESE TSUNAMI

JAPAN

MARCH 11, 2011

On March 11, 2011, a 9.0-magnitude earthquake struck Japan, setting off a devastating tsunami that destroyed cities and left 27,000 people dead, or missing. It was the strongest quake to hit the region since people started keeping records almost 150 years ago. While the loss of life was staggering, the tsunami damaged atomic power plants, triggering a nuclear nightmare that threatened to poison the environment for generations. It was the worst crisis to hit Japan since World War II.

Japan and earthquakes are synonymous. The country sits atop the deadliest section in the 'Ring of Fire', an area in the Pacific where several of the Earth's tectonic plates continually shove against one another. The March 11 quake struck at 2.46 p.m. Tokyo time, shaking skyscrapers, toppling furniture, and snapping highways. Moments later, a tsunami rushed inland with a wall of water 30 feet high. The waves carried away homes, buildings, boats, buses and factories. Thousands ran for higher ground.

The damage was incomprehensible. Thousands of bodies littered the landscape. The waves carried others out to sea. Unbelievably, the death toll could have been greater, but Japan has strict building codes designed to minimize earthquake damage. Moreover, the earthquake hit far from Japan's industrial heartland, which spared its economy.

Despite the devastation, there were many stories of survival. Six hundred people escaped the rushing water by climbing to the roof of a grade school in Sendai City, near the epicenter of the quake. One man was found days later hanging on to the roof of a house that floated far out to sea.

In the city of Iwanuma, doctors and nurses ran to the rooftop of Chuo Hospital, waving white flags and pink umbrellas. On the floor of the roof they spelled out "Help" in English, and "Food" in Japanese. As people frantically searched for loved ones and tried to find food and shelter, a larger, more ominous disaster was taking shape. The earthquake and tsunami had heavily damaged the Fukushima Daiichi nuclear plant where explosions rocked four buildings that housed six nuclear reactors. Spent fuel rods stored in some of the buildings began melting down, releasing dangerous amounts of radioactivity.

Thirty-hours after the quake, the government imposed a 12-mile evacuation zone around the facility. More than 78,000 people lived in the zone before the earthquake and tsunami hit. Many rushed to find shelter at evacuation centers. They had no time to gather their valuables.

As the crisis progressed, a small group of workers spent weeks trying to bring the nuclear crisis under control. They worked feverishly to stabilize the Fukushima Daiichi plant, including pumping in sea water to cool the spent fuel rods. Workers were also forced to dump radioactive water into the ocean.

Clean up after the devastation was monumental. The U.S. military and others worked alongside the Japanese Self Defense Forces. They brought in heavy equipment, supplies, food and medicine.

AT A GLANCE

An earthquake measuring 8.8 on the Richter scale jolted off the east coast of Japan's main Honshu island on March 11, 2001. More than 27,000 people are feared dead or missing.